Why Not Wisconsin?

From Barry to Bo:
Broadcasting the Badgers
from the Best Seat in the House

Matt Lepay

TRIUMPH
B O O K S

Library of Congress Cataloging-in-Publication Data

Lepay, Matt, 1962–
  Why not Wisconsin? : from Barry to Bo, broadcasting the Badgers from the best seat in the house / Matt Lepay.
       p. cm.
  Includes bibliographical references and index.
  ISBN 978-1-60078-705-8
1. University of Wisconsin-Madison—Football—History. 2. Wisconsin Badgers (Football team)—History. 3. University of Wisconsin-Madison—Basketball—History. 4. Wisconsin Badgers (Basketball team)—History. I. Title.
  GV958.U5867L46 2012
  796.332'630977583—dc23

                                                                2012019667

This book is available in quantity at special discounts for your group or organization. For further information, contact:

    Triumph Books LLC
    814 North Franklin Street
    Chicago, Illinois 60610
    Phone: (312) 337-0747
    www.triumphbooks.com

Printed in U.S.A.
ISBN: 978-1-60078-705-8
Design by Sue Knopf
Photos courtesy of AP Images unless otherwise indicated

To my parents, Lee and Salvador,
who always encouraged me to pursue my dreams.

To my brother, Tom, and my sister, Denise,
for putting up with their little brother.

To Linda, the love of my life
who also happens to be a far superior writer.
I look forward to reading your book.

Contents

Foreword

IN THE CRAZY BUSINESS OF TV SPORTS, there are times when you think you have seen it all. Then you find yourself involved in the most important college football game of the week—in Tokyo, Japan! And when it's over, you are in the winning coach's hotel room, cocktail in hand, sharing the day's memories of Wisconsin's win that had just clinched a spot in the "Granddaddy of 'Em All," the Rose Bowl.

That is exactly what I was doing late into the evening of December 4, 1993. The year before, the Badgers had given up a home date to play Michigan State in the final game of the regular season. Win, and Wisconsin would be headed to Pasadena for the first time in 31 years. They would play the game 6,000 miles from home. For me, it was a chance to witness history on a road trip to the other side of the world.

It was a local broadcast crew, for the most part. So there was an occasional appearance by a sideline reporter speaking Japanese. And the cameraman in our booth fell asleep during the game. I doubt many fans at the Tokyo Dome that night knew or even cared what was at stake, but after the Badgers had beaten the Spartans, there was not a happier man in Japan than Barry Alvarez.

Count me among those who have had good seats to watch the growth of University of Wisconsin athletics. In the early-to-mid 1990s, my old broadcast partner, Gary Danielson, and I felt like we were, at least, semi-regular announcers for Badgers football, be it at Camp Randall Stadium in Madison or some other Big Ten city.

Being from the Midwest, I was aware of Wisconsin's sporting history or at times lack thereof. I knew that when most people thought of the Big Ten, it was usually the Big Two, Ohio State and Michigan. When Pat Richter hired Barry Alvarez in January 1990, however, that landscape changed.

Naturally, in my play-by-play role with ABC/ESPN, I never pull for one team over another. But I will admit I am happy when good things happen to good people. As I travel across the country in this job, I can say I've developed a number of friendships. Among the closest of those relationships are with Barry Alvarez and Bret Bielema.

For the past 20 years, I have hosted a golf tournament in my hometown in Minnesota. The Nessler Memorial is named after my late father, Bob. All the money raised goes to cancer research, and both Barry and Bret have been kind enough to headline the event. Trust me when I say how much that has meant to my family. In fact, they've become part of our family in St. Charles.

But well beyond that example, I have found all the folks at the UW to be great people. From Barry, Bret, Pat, and the basketball coaches like Dick Bennett and Bo Ryan, I have always looked forward to being assigned a Badgers game and spending time in "Madtown." They are good people who also happen to be really good at what they do. There are times when I watch their teams and question their chances to win, but year in and year out, they find a way, and there they are again, playing in the major bowl games and making noise in the NCAA Tournament.

Make no mistake—this is one of the better stories in college sports. I'm glad I was around to witness it and be part of it. Like I said, I'm not allowed to cheer, but when Wisconsin does well, I allow myself a smile. I know my Badgers sports family has had another good day.

Brad Nessler
ABC/ESPN/NFLN

Introduction: For Openers

LET US START WITH THIS BOOK'S TITLE, which might sound familiar to a few Badger fans. Why not Wisconsin? They are three words that go hand-in-hand with Joe Panos, an All-American offensive lineman who helped lead the University of Wisconsin to its first-ever Rose Bowl victory. Nearly 20 years later, those words continue to have great meaning. Joe helped create an attitude that the Badgers could compete with anyone. You can respect your opponent. Just never fear them. Players such as Joe Panos are what the Wisconsin Badgers are all about. When I asked him if we could "borrow" his words for the title of this book, he quickly and graciously approved. For the younger fan, I just want to make sure you know where "Why not Wisconsin?" originated.

While this project will focus on Wisconsin football and basketball from 1988 through 2011, Badger fans should always understand that the tradition of these programs goes back a long way. Through the years, I have made countless mistakes, including going through a period where I largely ignored the history of these teams. Yes, the Badgers football squad won its first Rose Bowl in 1994, and the basketball team went 47 years between postseason bids, but those who are old enough, and those who are wise enough, are well aware of some of the great players who created lasting memories at Camp Randall Stadium and the UW Field House.

There are many factors that make this job so enjoyable. One of them is getting to know some of the UW athletes who performed before my arrival in Madison. An obvious name is Pat Richter; some of the others from that era include Dale Hackbart and Jim Bakken. I remember Jim from his days as a kicker with the St. Louis Cardinals. Now I know him as a good man who can still drive the ball well off the tee and usually right down the middle of the fairway.

Stu Voigt is one of the greatest athletes in Madison, Wisconsin, sports history. I first recognized his name from his career with the Minnesota Vikings. Now I see him a few times a year at various UW and charity outings, and we always have a nice chat.

Bill Marek is one of the greatest running backs in Wisconsin history, and clearly he was one of the Big Ten's best backs in the 1970s.

In the 1980s, the Badgers had a safety tandem of Matt VandenBoom and David Greenwood. Matt had a dream game against No. 1 Michigan in 1981, when he intercepted three passes to help lead the Badgers to an opening day upset. Greenwood was a crazy-good athlete who is now a golf pro in Florida.

It is a similar story with basketball. I am not sure you will meet a nicer person than Rick Olson. You might also be hard-pressed to find a better shooter. If only the three-point shot was in play throughout his college career. The man could stroke it. He works for Mueller Sports Medicine in Wisconsin, and it is always fun to catch up with him.

Speaking of Mueller Sports, the head guy there is none other than Kurt Mueller, also known as Mutumbo. For those who watch Badgers home basketball games, he is the one with the curly blond hair, often times wearing leather pants while he "helps" the officials from his courtside seat. He also has been very generous in his support of the University of Wisconsin.

Ab Nicholas has been quite successful in the financial world. He and his charming wife, Nancy Johnson, also have been extremely important contributors to the university. Among their gifts was their support for the Nicholas-Johnson Pavilion and Plaza, which is the practice gym in the Kohl Center. It should be noted that Ab could play a little hoops, too. In 1951 and '52, he was All–Big Ten.

On February 12, 2011, the Badgers rallied from 15 points down to beat No. 1 Ohio State. The honorary captain that day was former coach John Erickson, whose team knocked off the top-ranked Buckeyes in March 1962. It was a treat visiting with him again, and it was fun to notice how much he still enjoys keeping tabs on the Badgers.

The list could go on and on. My point is that while this project is about the growth of the University of Wisconsin programs, it is my hope that Badgers fans will always remember those who played long before 1988. Yes, there were tough years. Sometimes there were long stretches of tough years. But make no mistake—there were many great players who put on some incredible displays in their time. It is pretty special to know that so many of those talented men continue to have such an interest in how today's teams are doing.

Since 1988, many things have changed. The average cost of a gallon of gas was $1.08. A new home went for about $138,000. We knew nothing about the Internet, and the term "social media" was years away from becoming part of our vocabulary.

Much has changed in the world of University of Wisconsin athletics since 1988. Today, fans expect the football team to play not just in bowl games, but in high-profile bowl games. Fans are used to seeing the basketball squad in the NCAA Tournament every year, and Big Ten titles no longer seem to be a surprise.

I have had the opportunity to broadcast hundreds of football and basketball games. In 1988, I worked with Larry Mialik on UW football broadcasts. We were one of four Wisconsin radio crews before the school went to an exclusive carrier the following season. From 1989 until 1993, I handled pregame, halftime, and postgame duties for all but two games before becoming the team's play-by-play announcer in 1994.

Since the 1988–89 season, I have had the privilege of calling UW basketball games. For the first six seasons, I worked with Ron Blomberg. "The Professor" is the very definition of class. He picked up the nickname courtesy of his former broadcast partner, the legendary voice of the Milwaukee Bucks, Eddie Doucette.

Since 1994, I have been alongside Mike Lucas, who has covered UW athletics for more than four decades. He is a walking encyclopedia of Badgers sports history.

Together, we have had an amazing opportunity to watch a pair of programs grow to heights that might have seemed impossible but have become very real. Along the way there have been more than a few interesting stories. Some are funny, while others have helped me gain at least some perspective on what players and coaches deal with while performing on a big stage.

We hope you enjoy reliving some memories from someone who has never scored a point, blocked anyone, or even set a screen, but has been lucky enough to have the best seat in the house.

1

Never Underestimate the Power of Good Timing

ONE OF MY FAVORITE SAYINGS comes from former UW basketball coach Dick Bennett, who leaned on these four words quite a bit during his stellar career: "Know who you are." This means know your strengths, and know where you can improve. I consider myself someone with a rather limited skill set. Like many young boys, I had dreams of being a professional athlete. My fantasy was to play for the Cincinnati Reds. I grew up spoiled rotten, watching the Big Red Machine of Pete Rose, Joe Morgan, Johnny Bench, Tony Perez, and all the other terrific players who made up one of Major League Baseball's best-ever teams.

However, try as I might, I realized in high school that the odds of me ever getting paid to play baseball were slim and none. Make that none and laugh-out-loud-and-please-leave-the-room none. Basketball also was out of the question. As for football, well, that wasn't going to happen, either. I had the double-curse—I wasn't very big, but I was slow. To be fair, I also broke my leg playing baseball on a muddy field. I was playing second base. While I was covering the base on a steal attempt, an errant throw forced me to the first-base side of the bag, and I collided with the runner. My leg got caught in the muck, and snap! Down goes Lepay.

1

To make a long, boring story a little shorter, my leg was not properly healing. During basketball training camp the next fall, I was unable to run very well, even by my rather low standards. I needed a bone graft operation; doctors took some bone from my right hip to help my right tibia heal. As they were performing the surgery, they discovered a fist-sized tumor, which luckily was benign. The operation went well, but I had to go more than a year without running, jumping, or putting any kind of stress on the leg.

I could say that stopped a great athletic career from unfolding, but I would be lying. I have always loved playing sports, especially baseball and basketball, but someone of my limited ability was going to peak early, like about 6th grade. I go back to Bennett's line "Know who you are." By the time I was in high school, I knew I was never going to possess the physical ability to play at a high level. Coaching was something I thought about, but early in life I contracted a bug. It just happened to be the broadcasting bug. I grew up listening to Reds games on the radio with Al Michaels. Yes, *that* Al Michaels. Before he hit it big on the national stage, he was the Voice of the Cincinnati Reds. Following the 1973 season, he left that gig to become the San Francisco Giants announcer. In Cincinnati, a young announcer named Marty Brennaman arrived, and he has been the team's primary radio voice ever since.

I loved, and in fact still love, how good announcers describe a game, especially on the radio. While baseball obviously warrants a different tempo from football and basketball, my desire to get into this racket began with Al Michaels and Marty Brennaman. Of course, to many sports fans, Michaels is best known for his call of the 1980 U.S. Olympic hockey team's improbable run to the gold medal in Lake Placid. "Do you believe in miracles? Yes!" might be the most famous line in sports broadcasting history.

For me, Michaels has another line that runs a close second. In the 1972 National League Championship Series, the Reds and Pirates were battling in the fifth and decisive game. Going into the bottom of the ninth, Pittsburgh led 3–2. Johnny Bench tied the game with an opposite-field home run. Later in the inning, with George Foster at third, Hal McRae at the plate, and Bob Moose on the mound, I had my first real moment of what heaven is like for a sports fan. Almost 40 years later, I clearly remember Michaels' call. "The 1–1 pitch to McRae—in the dirt—it's a wild pitch! Here comes Foster! The Reds win the pennant!!" (Michaels pauses as the crowd goes wild.) "Bob Moose throws a wild pitch, and the Reds have won the National League pennant!"

Sports nuts across the country have terrific memories for such moments. We might forget our home address, but we remember great games by our favorite teams. That was mine, and I was just 10 years old, but I knew at some point I wanted to have a job like Al Michaels. I like to think that my lack of athletic ability helped to accelerate the process.

While attending Ohio State University (note I am refraining from writing The Ohio State University), my focus shifted from baseball to college football and basketball. I set a goal of being the voice of a major college program within five years of graduation. I made it, but it was more because of dumb luck than anything else.

While in school, a group of us put together broadcasts of OSU hockey and baseball games. We actually went out and sold enough advertising to cover the costs of phone lines and even some travel. Since we were just a campus radio station that about 50 people could actually hear, we knew those advertisers were very sympathetic.

We had no real guidance. We just called the games as best we could and hoped to get a demo together to help us find a job after graduation. It worked well enough for me to get hired by WNCI in Columbus, which at the time was owned by Nationwide, the insurance folks. Our studio was downtown in, oddly enough, the Nationwide building. It was quite the contrast, insurance folks wearing gray suits and white shirts, working in the same building as a bunch of knuckleheads at a radio station playing Top 40 music.

WNCI was, and still is, a music station, so play-by-play was not going to happen. I went from being a news and sports reporter to the morning drive sports anchor. Eventually I became the morning news and sports anchor. I wasn't very good, but I did get a good education into the business of radio. Not long after I started, the station fired its longtime morning personality, which created quite a stir in the local radio world.

There is an old saying about broadcasting—"You haven't lived until you've been fired." By early spring of 1986, I could say that I lived. Our station had tweaked its format a few times and hired and fired various DJs. Now it was my turn. The program director called me into his office, and with all the warmth of a January blizzard said, "Matt, we have to cut the budget. That means we have to let you go." After directing me to the business office to get my last check, he offered me this lovely parting gift. "I have to write a memo on this. Do you want me to say you resigned or that we let you go?" I opted for the latter. I believe my dismissal saved the station a grand total of about $12,000. Big bucks in the big city, right?

It probably was the best thing that could have happened. I was reading news and sports and yukking it up with the morning host of the moment. There is nothing wrong with that, but I wanted to call games, and that was not going to happen at WNCI.

After a brief stint as a news director in Athens, Ohio, I finally was able to land a job that allowed me to do some play-by-play. At WPTW in Piqua (pronounced Pick-wa), Ohio, we called a ton of area high school football and basketball games, as well as some American Legion baseball. That was the good part. The radio version of purgatory was that we pulled eight-hour air shifts playing the "beautiful music of yesteryear." It was elevator music. I had gone from a station that played Phil Collins, Madonna, and Huey Lewis to a station that played "I'm Just a Singer in a Rock 'N Roll Band" by something called 101 Strings with Trumpet.

After close to two years of that, I figured maybe this radio thing might not work out. My girlfriend and future wife Linda (same person, by the way) was already working in Columbus, and we thought it would be a good idea to return to school, pick up a few more public relations classes, and get a job in the world of PR.

This is where I got lucky. The day I resigned, I picked up a trade publication called *Broadcasting* magazine. In the classified section was an ad for an afternoon drive sports anchor and play-by-play announcer for Wisconsin basketball. I put together an audition tape, mailed it to WTSO radio in Madison, and since I knew next to nothing about Badger basketball, I started doing a little research.

It was as though the planets aligned. Within a few days, I received a call from Chris Moore, who was the station's sports director, morning drive anchor, hockey announcer and, when needed, an all-around nut job who could crack up a room with his humor. Within two weeks, the station brought Linda and I to Madison, where we met Chris, as well as program director Jeff Tyler and station manager Roger Russell. My head was spinning, but Russell did a lot to put me at ease. He was a very folksy but savvy radio man. People seemed to actually enjoy coming to work every day, which is something I did not experience at a couple of my previous stops. Rog's first question was, "So, you like to fish?" followed by, "Do you golf? What's your handicap?" I figured he knew I was pretty nervous, so he was just trying to put me at ease. Others have told me he did this quite a bit when he interviewed job candidates.

They offered me the job on the spot, which is something that does not happen very often. Linda and I talked it over, and within two days of the interview, we were getting ready to move to Wisconsin. In just a few short weeks, our life plans had changed. We were nervous about leaving Ohio. Adding to our little angst was the fact that, out of the blue, Linda had a job offer in San

Diego. So not only were we leaving our family and friends in Ohio, we turned down a chance to live in Southern California, all so I could pursue my dream of being a major college play-by-play announcer.

Our biggest worries about moving to Wisconsin were probably similar to others who grew up south of there. How much snow do you guys get? Will my car survive the sub-zero temperatures? Did we *really* just say no to a job offer in San Diego? Okay, maybe not everyone asks that last question, but it was going through our minds.

Chris Moore was a huge help. The only problem was three months after we moved to Madison, he left. Chris is a very gifted broadcaster, and he is also funny as hell. He does a great Dick Vitale impression, and he had a number of other character voices that came in handy during his sports updates for WTSO and also WZEE (Z104), a highly rated Top 40 station. Chris was able to chase his dream of becoming an NHL broadcaster, and he left Madison for the New Jersey Devils. He later became the voice of the Florida Panthers. From there, Moore went on to stints with ESPN and Fox Sports Radio. He lives on the East Coast now, and his wife, Pam, is a successful attorney.

Chris could tell Linda and I had reservations about moving to Wisconsin, and he went out of his way to make us feel comfortable. Maybe many of you have no idea who Chris Moore is, but I will say without hesitation that any success I have had in this business is in large part because of Chris. He discovered my demo tape and was very aggressive in giving a 26-year-old know-nothing a shot at calling major college basketball games.

Life takes people in different directions, and it has been too long since I have talked to Chris, but for Badger fans who like what I do, credit Chris. Of course, if you wish I had never arrived in Madison, I would suggest it is all Chris Moore's fault. Feel free to blame him!

Little did we know in June 1988 that when we moved here from Ohio, that I would end up with a pretty cool gig. Through the years, I would find out that the planets would align several more times, making me as lucky as any sports announcer in Wisconsin, and perhaps beyond.

Thank you again, Chris, for taking a few minutes to listen to my audition tape.

2
First Impressions

TODAY, CAMP RANDALL STADIUM HAS SUITES, club seats, and nice scoreboards with video screens, not to mention statues of Pat Richter and Barry Alvarez. There is also a phallic-looking sculpture called Nails Tails, which stands erect, so to speak, outside the stadium near the southwest corner of a small parking lot. As you might guess, Nails Tails has been the target of many one-liners since its unveiling in 2005.

No matter what you might think of Nails Tails, the stadium looks pretty good these days. It has come a long way from the Camp Randall I walked into for the first time in June 1988. Back then the stadium, while nearly a quarter century younger, looked much older. The artificial surface was about as soft as your average driveway. There were no statues to be found. The offices were creaky. It certainly was not what anyone would expect from a major college program.

It is a similar story of compare and contrast between the Kohl Center today and the UW Field House. The Kohl Center is a huge, 17,000 seat arena for basketball, and it holds more than 15,000 for hockey. It has hosted major non-sports related events from Elton John to the Dalai Lama. While maybe not the most intimate building in the world, it has been a very good home for Wisconsin basketball and hockey.

Meanwhile, the Field House has been remodeled and today serves as a good home for volleyball and wrestling, but when I

9

walked into the old barn back in the summer of '88, I have to say it was underwhelming. Among other things, it was in need of a paint job and new windows. Depending on where you were sitting, you could be freezing or boiling.

Or you might be hacking up a lung.

In the late 1980s, you could still smoke in the concourse. For many, that was a halftime ritual, which made a radio broadcaster's job a bit more challenging. Our location was Row 1 of the upper level. Keeping in mind that smoke rises, you can imagine what the Field House was like for those of us who were seated upstairs.

It also was plenty warm up there, until someone opened a window or unless someone sat by a broken window. In addition, it was a good idea to take care of your bathroom needs before tip-off. Similar to Williams Arena at Minnesota now, restrooms at the Field House were lacking. I often had nightmares of standing in a line 100 people deep at halftime and missing the start of the second half. Suffice it to say it was a good idea for me to go easy on the sodas before game time.

However, I always like to have some water handy during a broadcast. At the Field House, that got me in trouble more than once. Being in the upper level means there are fans sitting right below me. We are talking about bleacher seats, so if I drop something, it lands on someone in the lower level. A couple of times I accidentally knocked a cup of water off my ledge that passed for a table, and some fan would get an unexpected bath. On one occasion, the fan decided to march right up to my spot, and while I was on the air, he began to chew me out for being a klutz. I had to admit that I could not blame him. I was just thankful he didn't douse me with a full cup of soda.

Maybe time makes the memories grow fonder, but I kind of miss those old Field House days. I believe the fans who were there truly loved the game. Although I said my first visit was underwhelming, I will say that when the place was full, it rocked. There were days or nights after really good games when I would leave the building with my ears ringing. Man, can those old buildings hold noise.

I think players, especially good shooters, really enjoyed playing there. The place is intimate, providing a good shooting background. In a book he wrote many years ago, Steve Alford mentioned how much he liked playing in those types of gyms. For those who only know Alford as a coach, I'll just say that as a star at Indiana University, he could shoot the ball a little.

Although Camp Randall looked a little beat up by 1988, I could imagine how that stadium must have been during great football games such as when the Badgers upset No. 1 Michigan in 1981 or when they knocked off Ohio State in 1984. When I first arrived in town, I heard an audio clip from the great announcer Earl Gillespie as he described a fourth-down stop that sealed a 16–14 victory. "Byars is short!! Byars is short!!" referring to star Buckeyes running back Keith Byars. It was hard not to get goosebumps listening to Gillespie's classic voice with the roar of the crowd in the background.

Unfortunately, there were far more snores than roars in the fall of 1988. I was struck by the lack of anticipation going into the season. It did not take very long to understand why. The football team had produced three straight losing seasons. In the spring of 1986, Coach Dave McClain died of a heart attack. Jim Hilles had the difficult task of trying to lead the Badgers that fall, and the team finished 3–9.

Enter Don Morton. He could talk a pretty good game, and no doubt he excited boosters and other fans across the state. It was even better when Wisconsin beat Hawaii in the 1987 season opener. After winning two of three non-conference games, reality set in with a 1–7 Big Ten record. At least the one victory was against Ohio State, so at the time the program could try to hang its hat on that victory.

Only the public wasn't buying it anymore. By 1988, year two of the three-season Morton Era, the opener against Western Michigan drew a crowd of 38,230. That meant there were about 40,000 empty seats at Camp Randall. The "empty seat crowd" looked pretty smart as the Badgers lost 24–14. I just wasn't used to seeing this at a college football game. I had grown accustomed to packed crowds eagerly awaiting the kickoff at Ohio State.

In those days, part of the pregame festivities included the Bucky Wagon, which was an old fire engine with cheerleaders on board. The Bucky Wagon would roll down the north end-zone tunnel, and back in the day, that really got the crowd going. However, by September 1988, the Bucky Wagon and the team running out on the field got a reaction that reminded me of the pep rally scene from the movie *Fast Times at Ridgemont High*. Remember? The cheerleaders tried to get the student body fired up for the big game, only nobody in the student body cared?

It was a shame, because there were some very good players on that team—just not nearly enough. Guys such as Don Davey, who would go on to become a four-time Academic All-American, and Troy Vincent, who had a very good NFL career and was named to the Pro Bowl five times. Other players of note included Dan Kissling, Tim Knoeck, Brady Pierce, Chad VandeZande, Todd Nelson, Jim Basten, and a tight end named Paul Chryst.

I never had any personal problems with Don Morton. Actually, I liked the man, but clearly Morton and Wisconsin made for a very bad match. It did not take long in that 1988 season for things to start turning ugly. Clashes with some media members became personal. Morton made a poor PR move on his weekly television show when he opened a program by rising from a casket, claiming, "We're not dead yet."

The first road game that season was in Miami to play the Hurricanes at the Orange Bowl. Jimmy Johnson's bunch. "The U." It was a typical tropical day in South Florida, nearly 90 degrees with humidity to match. Earlier in the morning, there had been a fire in the press box, so it was hot, muggy, and smoky. The game itself was nondescript. The previous week Miami had beaten Michigan 31–30, and it was a couple of weeks away from a showdown with Notre Dame in the famous matchup billed as "Catholics vs. Convicts." The 'Canes went through the motions and beat the Badgers 23–3. After the game as I walked out of the stadium, there was Jimmy Johnson, with a cold, tall beer in each hand. Right then I knew I liked this guy. I seem to remember that more than the game itself.

In many ways that '88 season was summed up during a home game against Illinois. In a promotion to try to get some fans, any fans, into the stadium, the UW drummed up something called Circus Day. At halftime there was a mini circus show, complete with elephants and all the rest. Well, a couple of the elephants must not have had a chance to take care of some personal business after breakfast, if you know what I mean. As a result, a couple of the circus animals relieved themselves on the field. My current broadcast partner and longtime sportswriter Mike Lucas referred to one of them as Binky the All Bran Elephant. Is that too much information?

Anyway, little did Larry Mialik and I know we would have to fill time before the second-half kickoff because workers had to clean up elephant crap and hose down the field.

We came out of a commercial break, and I gave some first half statistics. Suddenly, I heard Mialik start to laugh. We both noticed what was going on, and now we both were laughing. Then we start a little banter.

"Let me put it this way," I started. "They've brought elephants on the field, and the worst fears were confirmed. If anyone has a shovel and is near Camp Randall, we could use your help."

"There is going to be a slippery spot on about the 50, in front of the Badger bench," Larry added.

"As well as in the end zone by the Field House."

"They dotted the 'I' [in Wisconsin]."

"The fans have something to talk about, no matter what happens in the second half."

"Yes sir, Circus Day at Camp Randall," Larry noted, and then he tried to add a positive spin to the mess, reminding listeners that UW officials are looking into replacing the old artificial turf anyway.

"They could just go ahead and do that now," I concluded, thinking to myself, *What a first season this is turning out to be.*

They cleaned up elephant mess, but the game itself only got worse. A 7–6 Illinois lead at the half turned into a 34–6 Illini victory. One bad pile just led to another.

The 1988 season ended with an unsightly 36–0 loss at Michigan State. The next week I bumped into a couple of players who told me the Spartans knew exactly what plays the Badgers were running. "*They* were telling *me* what the play was going to be," a lineman said.

Going back to the end of the 1987 season, the Badgers dropped 11 straight games. To put it another way, they went one year and six days between victories. The one game they did win was against Minnesota, in the annual Battle for Paul Bunyan's Axe. It was an ugly game. Mialik and I would just look at each other and roll our eyes between plays.

After the game, the Badgers were able to take a victory lap with the Axe. What I remember most from that day is when a player named Jeff Weyker got the Axe in his hands. Jeff could get rather animated, and for a few seconds we thought the south-end goal post would not survive. Weyker started chopping at it pretty hard, but he eventually gave up the Axe to a teammate.

The goalpost remained standing, but Morton would only last one more year as the Badgers coach. Before that first season, people told me how Wisconsin football was such a big event. Even if the team struggled, Camp Randall was the scene of a pretty good party on a nice fall Saturday. That first year it became obvious that the party was leaving town.

I hosted Morton's radio call-in show, and even that started to get nasty. Fans were angry. They wanted to know how in the world could Morton's veer offense fit with the current personnel, and would the Badgers ever again be competitive in the Big Ten?

Then the worst thing that can happen in sports started to occur. Fans went from anger to apathy, as was evidenced by the lack of occupied seats for home games. That was my first season covering Wisconsin football. Making matters worse for football fans in this state was that the Packers stunk, too, making for a very long first autumn for a young broadcaster from Ohio. Yes, I was wondering, *What in the world did I get myself into here?*

But thanks to basketball, that first season covering Wisconsin athletics had its good moments. Actually, there were quite a few big moments that season. Maybe most people would not identify it as great, but it turned out to be a very important year in the growth of Badger basketball.

Perhaps I did wonder what I was doing in Madison, Wisconsin. I had no way of knowing that I was going to have an amazingly good seat to witness the rise of two programs. Not many people were thinking that way in the late 1980s. Luckily for Badger sports fans, there were a few who believed the University of Wisconsin could excel not only academically but athletically, as well.

3

A Very Important Team

I HAVE TO ADMIT THAT PRIOR TO MOVING TO MADISON, my knowledge of all things Wisconsin basketball was minimal. Growing up, I was a big fan of the University of Dayton Flyers. Coach Don Donoher had some terrific teams, and one of their rivalry games was with Marquette, so I knew far more about the Warriors (yes, I know, they are the Golden Eagles now, but I remember them as Warriors) than the Badgers.

I vividly remember a line in a preview magazine about the Badgers. "They are hoping to make the NCAA Tournament this season, something they have not done in the '80s. Nor did they make the NCAA Tournament in the 1970s. Nor did they make the NCAA Tournament in the '60s or in the '50s, either."

I had not realized that the Badgers had not made the "Big Dance" since 1947.

Let me stop right here. While the Badgers had many years where they simply were not very good, there were teams that by today's standards would have been tournament worthy. Those teams included the 1961–62 Badgers of Coach John Erickson, who thumped No. 1 Ohio State 86–67. I also would throw the 1973–74 Badgers into the tournament. John Powless led his squad to a 16–8 overall record, and it finished fourth in the Big Ten.

Yet the fact remained that while the Badgers clearly had some excellent players through the years, losing records were the rule rather than the exception. Heading into the 1988–89 season, Wisconsin was trying to snap an eight-year streak of .500 or sub-.500 basketball.

It is probably safe to say that the masses were not counting down the days until the first game, but there was some intrigue about that team during training camp. Players such as Danny Jones and Trent Jackson were established threats. Sophomore Tim Locum was in the early stages of becoming one of the school's best-ever three-point shooters. Add some flash from Willie "Ice" Simms and the steady nature of guard Tom Molaski, and there was reason to believe the Badgers would at least be decent.

The year started well enough as Wisconsin won nine of its first ten games, including the Big Ten opener against Minnesota. A four-game losing streak followed, including an overtime heart-breaker to Indiana 61–58. For Badger fans, this probably was not as crushing at the epic triple-overtime loss two years earlier, but the frustration of constantly losing to Bob Knight's Hoosiers was evident, even to a first-year college radio announcer. That was the 17th straight meeting that Indiana defeated the Badgers. The streak stretched to 31 before Dick Bennett's Badgers finally stopped the bleeding in 1997.

After the three-point loss in January 1989, a little magic started happening at the UW Field House, beginning with a game against Michigan. This is the same Michigan team that went on to win the national title, with Rumeal Robinson hitting two big free throws in the championship game. On January 21 of that season, I had the chance to call my first really big Badger victory, and it came against that Wolverines team. At the time, Michigan was ranked sixth in the AP poll, but Wisconsin went toe-to-toe with them. At the half, the game was tied at 35. In the final minute, it was 68–68. Then, with 30 seconds to play, Trent Jackson drove to the bucket and was fouled. He made the first free throw to give Wisconsin a 69–68 lead. He then missed the second foul shot, but Michigan failed to secure the rebound and lost the ball out of bounds.

With 16 seconds remaining, Michigan fouled Tom Molaski, sending him to the line for a pressure-packed one-and-one. He missed the front end, and the Wolverines Loy Vaught grabbed the rebound. Would Wisconsin lose another heartbreaker? It appeared that way when Jackson fouled Robinson with :09 to play, sending the Michigan guard to the free throw line for two shots.

He was short with his first attempt. "Knew it when he released it," I said.

Robinson also missed his second free throw, but Terry Mills grabbed the board. However, Tim Locum was able to strip the ball from Mills, as I shrieked on the air. Locum was fouled, and with :03 showing on the clock, it was his turn for a critical one-and-one. Locum then had to wait for what seemed like three or four minutes while the officials determined whether to put another couple of seconds on the clock. They did, but Locum calmly drained the free throws, and Wisconsin had a signature victory 71–68.

The Badgers also would dispose of eighth-ranked Iowa 65–54 and had one of the Big Ten's top performances in a 72–52 trouncing of fifth-ranked Illinois. Trent Jackson poured in 27 points, Danny Jones added 17, while Tim Locum stuck four three-pointers. On the day, Wisconsin shot 57 percent from the field and 9-of-10 from long range. After building a 14 point lead at the half, Illinois never cut the deficit to less than 12 the rest of the way. Keep in mind just how good the Big Ten was that year. The Illini joined Michigan in Seattle for that year's Final Four. The Hawkeyes and the Hoosiers also were Top 10 teams when the Badgers faced them.

I should note that Robinson more than made up for his missed free throws in Madison. With 3 seconds remaining in overtime in the NCAA Championship Game against Seton Hall, Robinson drained two from the foul line to give Michigan the title. No doubt it was a trade Robinson was more than willing to make.

In the Badgers' rise to a nationally respected program, they have had some outstanding scoring duos, such as Michael Finley/Rashard

Griffith and Kammron Taylor/Alando Tucker. In that 1988–89 season, the combo of Danny Jones and Trent Jackson was, and still is, the best in UW history, averaging 39.5 points per game—20.4 for Jones and 19.1 for Jackson.

I believe the schedule worked against the Badgers that season. Four of their last five regular season games were on the road at Michigan, Purdue, Indiana, and finally at Michigan State. Making the game in East Lansing even worse was that it was the final home game for the Spartans at Jenison Field House. Simply put, the deck was stacked against Steve Yoder's team. It lost those road games, beating only Ohio State in the Badgers' last home game. Imagine at that time concluding your season at Indiana, then closing down a building that men such as Magic Johnson, Greg Kelser, Scott Skiles, and others, including Coach Jud Heathcote, made famous.

The Badgers hung in there for a while—they actually led 31–28 at the half. Then Michigan State came alive, taking the lead for good one minute into the second half on a Kirk Manns three-pointer. Danny Jones led Wisconsin with 24 points, while Steve Smith matched him for the Spartans.

On Selection Sunday, many of us in the media joined Yoder at WISC-TV, the CBS station in Madison, for the tournament selection show. It was not quite as elaborate a production as it is today, but there was reason to show up at the station, just in case the Badgers still managed to get an NCAA bid. The overall record was a solid 18–12, but an 8–10 league mark with four losses in their last five games proved costly as the Badgers were denied a spot in the tournament. You could see the disappointment on Yoder's face. He knew this was his best chance yet for Wisconsin to make the field, but later that night we learned the Badgers would be in the NIT, making it the school's first postseason bid in men's basketball since 1947.

They ended up hosting two NIT games that season, beating a Tim Floyd–coached New Orleans team 63–61 before falling to St. Louis 73–68 in round two. Obviously, fans were hoping the team could make it to New York's Madison Square Garden for the NIT semi-finals and finals, but in many ways the 1988–89 season was a breakthrough.

I was a young announcer only four years older than the seniors, so it was a great experience. Danny Jones might not have been a big fan of doing media interviews, but he could flash a smile that would light up a room. Trent Jackson came a long way from a young man who at one point had a stuttering problem that made him understandably shy around people he did not know very well. He got some help and worked very hard, and after his college playing days were done it was hard for a lot of us to get him to shut up.

I'm just kidding about that part. A few years ago, Trent was working for the UW Foundation, and during summertime public relations events, he would entertain us with stories from his playing days. Actually, he would just start jaw-jacking about how good he was. He was joking around, but you know what? He was pretty darn good.

I especially enjoyed talking to Tim Locum. While some members of the team struggled to get used to the increased media demands, Locum was always generous with his time. In those days, we sometimes would conduct interviews before practice. Usually for TV and radio chats, players would just stand near the court and do the interview in two or three minutes. If they did not want to talk, they would just hang out in the locker room as long as they could before practice started. Then there was Locum. Tim would ask if we could sit down. The man just wanted to pace himself before another practice began. He never seemed to be in a big hurry to get on the practice floor, but once he did—man, could he shoot the ball.

Every now and then I bump into Tom Molaski and Darin Schubring. "Mo" had a very solid senior season. Never a big scorer, he averaged 3.6 assists a game and would grab two or three rebounds and make very smart decisions. Schubring was built like a tight end or maybe even a defensive end. He was really put together, and while people gave him a ton of grief about his free throw shooting, I always thought he was just the kind of tough guy any coach would love to have on his team. These two in particular really seem to be enjoying the success of Bo Ryan's Badgers. I believe that, like perhaps many others, they wonder what it would have been like to play for Bo.

I always felt a little bit for big man Kurt Portmann. Tall high school players usually deal with higher expectations than others, and the 6'11" Portmann from Sheboygan was no exception. Yoder, not to mention some fans, could be tough on him, but Kurt's statistics remained modest. Yet he was an important player on that year's team, especially after Patrick Tompkins had to sit out the second semester for academic reasons. To his credit, Tompkins got things squared away in the classroom, and by his senior season in 1990–91, he was an All Big Ten performer.

Willie "Ice" Simms averaged 6.3 points per game in 1988–89. Like Tompkins, Ice would also have a big senior year, which helped him become something of a legend in the CBA. He turned out to be really good at driving to the bucket and drawing fouls, averaging a bit better than six free throw attempts a game in his final year. He also was known for getting himself thrown out of a practice when he decked Locum with an impressive-looking punch. During the course of a long season, tempers can flare on the practice floor, and that is what happened in this case. I should add that Locum popped up right away and continued practice. I can't tell you for sure, but I would be willing to bet that Tim knocked down several three-point shots during the rest of the day.

I know there were times when Yoder wanted to punch Simms, and probably the other way around, but the two co-existed well enough. Media members liked Willie. He was nothing if not honest in expressing his feelings, from playing time to how he was used in the offense. The Badgers' late public address announcer Jack Rane loved to say Willie's nickname, Ice. Jack would give it some hang time, as in "basket by Willie Simms...Iccccccccccccceeeeeee!" It worked well; the fans loved it, and I think Willie did, too.

Sadly for Yoder, the Badgers were unable to build off that season. The 1989–90 team with Jones and Portmann as seniors went just 14–17. The following year they were back in the NIT, but then it was right back to sub-.500 basketball in the 1991–92 season. The UW eased out Yoder, with the coach appearing at the news conference with Athletics Director Pat Richter announcing there would be no new contract, although Yoder would finish the season.

At the time of the announcement, there were six games remaining. The news conference took place in late morning/early afternoon. That night Yoder was scheduled to do his weekly radio show. Talk about timing. After the news conference I thought I had better check to make sure he would actually show up. As I approached him, Yoder knew what was going on. "Hey Matt, I'm not coming to the station tonight," he said with a straight face. Then he broke into a smile, "I'll be there. Don't worry." I told him I was sorry about what happened. I liked working with him. Yes, he could be a little gruff at times, but he always treated me better than I deserved.

That night on his radio show, the coach did something he rarely if ever did in a public forum—he choked up. Among the callers was a young boy who told Yoder how much he enjoyed watching the Badgers, and that he was sorry Steve was not going to coach the team next year. The sometimes cranky and always blunt Steve Yoder the fans saw suddenly gave way to a coach whose eyes got all watery. He could barely speak. I stalled as much as I could, but it became obvious that a commercial break was needed. The old boy was genuinely touched by that phone call.

In the first game after Yoder's dismissal, the Badgers absolutely abused the Fab Five of Michigan 96–78. Sophomore guard Tracy Webster and freshman Michael Finley went off at the Wolverines expense. Finley dropped 30 points and grabbed 13 rebounds. Webster just missed a triple-double, scoring 10 points, dishing out 13 assists, and adding nine rebounds. Tracy's assist total that night gave him the school's single-season record, passing Mike Heineman. It was a show. For one night, the Badgers were a dominant Big Ten team. For one night, the Fab Five wore Cardinal and White. After the game a number of us gathered at one of Yoder's favorite watering holes, Babe's Bar and Grill, which, truth be told, was a spot where you could have found Yoder and yours truly after any number of radio shows.

That night there was quite a gathering, including some of Yoder's longtime friends in the area, as well as Barry Alvarez and a couple of his assistant coaches. Several media members stopped by, such as longtime *Wisconsin State Journal* columnist Tom Oates, and two beat reporters who covered UW basketball, Vic Feuerherd from the *State Journal* and Dennis Chaptman from the *Milwaukee Journal*. It was a long but very fun night. I will just say that on that evening, business at Babe's was quite good.

The celebration eventually ended, as did the season, with a five game losing streak. Still, while this movie had anything but a happy ending, Yoder's Badgers of 1988–89 can and should take some credit for the rise of Wisconsin basketball. That team won some very big games. On a campus where hockey ruled the winter, and rightfully so, the basketball program made a statement that it, too, could be a player, and there was reason to be excited to see a game at the Field House.

4
Changes in Attitudes

THE 1989 FOOTBALL SEASON STARTED POORLY and never really got much better. The opener was a rematch with Miami, and it marked the debut of Hurricanes coach Dennis Erickson. Jimmy Johnson had moved on to join Jerry Jones and the Dallas Cowboys. Erickson actually was in the mix for the Badgers' job that eventually went to Don Morton, but after two years and a 4–18 record, Morton's veer offense was just another four-letter word to be avoided in Wisconsin.

People may not remember, but that first game of the '89 season was an ABC showcase game with Keith Jackson and Bob Griese. Wisconsin took a 3–0 lead, courtesy of a Rich Thompson field goal. Then Miami scored the next 51 points to make Erickson's debut a grand success. Jackson and Griese tried to be kind, with the former Purdue and Miami Dolphins great commenting that Morton "is a very nice man." Finally, Jackson had to admit on the air that he just didn't feel a lot of excitement in Madison about the season.

That was an understatement. The games became secondary to the main story of whether the UW would actually make a move and start over with a new coach.

In the radio booth, 1989 marked the first year of exclusive rights broadcasting. With WTMJ as the flagship, the crew was Jim Irwin, Elroy Hirsch, and Brian Manthey. Yours truly handled pregame, halftime, and some postgame duties, as well as Morton's weekly radio show. The Badgers' only victories were against Toledo and Northwestern. The only close losses in Big Ten play were a 31–24 setback at home against Iowa and a 24–22 crusher at Minnesota that might have sealed Morton's fate.

There is a reason I would put Jim Irwin on the Mount Rushmore of Wisconsin broadcasters, if there was such a thing. He did what he could to stay upbeat while still telling the truth. We all knew the Badgers were going to be in for a long season, but nobody wanted the broadcast to sound like a wake. Jim did what he could to keep fans listening for as long as possible, but it could not have been easy. For me, a big thrill was doing a postgame segment with Elroy. Actually, I think my father got an even bigger kick out of it when I told him what I was doing. My dad grew up on the South Side of Chicago. He loved the White Sox and whoever might be playing the Cubs.

He also enjoyed watching the Chicago Rockets. Who were the Chicago Rockets, you ask? They played in the old All America Football Conference that existed from 1946–49. Three teams from that league, the Cleveland Browns, the Baltimore Colts, and the San Francisco 49ers, joined the NFL in 1950. Anyway, one of Elroy's pro football stops was with the Rockets, and my dad loves to talk about how he enjoyed watching Elroy play, so he was thrilled to hear I was "playing radio" with Elroy Hirsch.

Simply put, "Crazylegs" was a treat to work with. A lot of us referred to him as "America's Guest." His personality was such that everyone just wanted to be around him. People have said that Elroy rarely had to pay to play some of the country's best golf courses or eat at the finest restaurants. During his time as Wisconsin's athletics director, he made friends across the state during the numerous summertime golf outings and other such events. He defined the term "goodwill ambassador," and as anyone who knew him would tell you, Crazylegs knew how to have a good time.

I will never forget how well he treated me. Elroy will forever be a beloved figure at the University of Wisconsin as well as the

University of Michigan. He was a star for the Los Angeles Rams. He is a pro football Hall of Famer. He worked and played with Hollywood legends. And here I am in the booth with Elroy Hirsch, and he made me feel comfortable. You know how it can be sometimes when you are afraid to meet someone you respect so much, be it an athlete, an actor, or anyone else whose work you appreciate? Sometimes the meeting can be a letdown. Sometimes that person can be an All-American jerk. Not Elroy Hirsch. He could not have been nicer, and in an otherwise depressing season, Crazylegs helped make it bearable.

The same goes for Jim, who is best known for being the longtime voice of the Green Bay Packers, but for years he did the same for the Badgers and the Milwaukee Bucks. His schedule was crazy, but he never seemed to let it get him down. I will always remember how well he treated me. Jim's wife, Gloria, often made the trip to Madison for home football games, and the Irwins often offered me words of encouragement, which meant a lot to a young broadcaster.

I have to admit the games of 1989 are very fuzzy in my memory. What I do recall is the stress on Morton and the toll it took. There were times when I would walk into his office, and he would just be getting off the phone with a supporter, or sometimes another coach, anyone he thought might be able to help him save his job.

Finally, the ax, or axes, started to fall. First, the UW announced that athletics director, Ade Sponberg, would be relieved of his duties. Then, a few days after the Badgers ended their season with a 31–3 loss to Michigan State before an announced crowd of 29,776 (most people swear it was a much smaller gathering), Chancellor Donna Shalala announced the school was making a coaching change.

As the announcement was happening, I was alone in Morton's office. We did our radio show from there, and the equipment was still set up. By this time I had a good enough relationship with him that we could do a one-on-one interview even after a rather bad day. I am sure he also was not opposed to having a forum to give his thoughts on the matter of his dismissal. Morton had that forum with our radio audience as well as his own news conference. "I didn't know if I wanted to be a football coach or join the circus. In the last three weeks, I have had the opportunity to do both," he said.

With that, Morton moved on, and very early on New Year's Day 1990, word spread like wildfire that new athletics director Pat Richter was going to hire a defensive coordinator from Notre Dame—some hotshot assistant coach who also served under Hayden Fry at Iowa. To say the least, Barry Alvarez hit the ground running, and the brash young assistant wasted no time in establishing his territory with the now famous opening news conference line of, "You better get your season tickets now, because before long you won't be able to."

For a team that in the last three years had a record of 6–27 and barely 10,000 fans in the stands by late in the fourth quarter of the 1989 season finale, it was a big time, stick-your-chest-out, boastful statement. And it was exactly what the University of Wisconsin needed.

There was no question this guy was going to change the culture of the Badger football program. Right away signs were posted on the doors—"Football Related Business Only." Alvarez was introduced as the new coach on January 2. Very soon after, I received a call from the football office saying I needed to stop by and pick up our radio equipment. They were remodeling the office and Barry had no need for that stuff. The man was about business. He knew how to win, and I believe he thought he could build Rome in a day.

Spring practices were an eye opener for everyone, most importantly the players. It was all about tempo. There was no wasted time. It was worth watching just to see a first-year defensive coordinator named Dan McCarney drive his players. His specific area was defensive line, and he was relentless on those guys, but those who stuck around grew to love him. McCarney was one of those coaches who could at times seem to be brutal on the field, but by the end of practice he would put his arm around a player and offer words of encouragement. At night, guys would tell me McCarney would make prank phone calls to players. It was his way of keeping things light but perhaps at the same time making sure everyone was taking care of business.

I remember Barry being all wound up before the season opener against California. He was hoping for a huge crowd, and in retrospect, I thought he believed that first team could win at least a little more than it did. Try as he might, and he and his staff worked the state hard, from the campus on out, to try to generate some interest. It would be a very tough sell. That was evident even on his radio call-in show, which moved from the coach's office to our studios at WTSO radio in Madison.

When speaking to various groups, Barry and I often tell this story. Do you know how long a 60-minute call-in show seems when nobody is calling? Oh, my goodness, in that first season, those shows were painful. So we had to improvise, adapt, and overcome. Dan McCarney would call the show. He would be "Dan from Middleton." Bill Callahan, who was Barry's offensive line coach, would be "Bill from Sun Prairie." On and on it went. We just needed some people to call and offer up some encouragement or ask a question about a young player who was showing promise. Yes, ladies and gentlemen, sometimes radio shows need "plants" to help a program along. Now you know.

That first team went 1–10 overall, and 0–8 in Big Ten play. Often the Badgers would hang in there for a half, but they simply did not have the personnel to compete in the Big Ten. I vividly remember the game at Northwestern. It was a bit of a shootout, but to use a cliché, Wisconsin did not have enough bullets. The Badgers scored late to make the final count look closer than it was as Northwestern won 44–34. At that time I was handling postgame radio duties, which included interviewing Barry. If he had any doubts about how tough his new job was going to be, they seemed to disappear that day. After that game, I was waiting to interview him, and he was slumped on a bench in the coach's locker room. He then fired his cap across the room, just disgusted at what had happened on the field. Keep in mind that Alvarez was not used to losing. He was two years removed from a national championship at Notre Dame. The following year wasn't half bad, either, culminating with Notre Dame putting on a clinic in the Orange Bowl as the Irish dismantled Colorado.

The Badgers would dismantle no one in 1990, yet something interesting was happening. I will never forget the atmosphere at a practice leading up to the final game of the year at Michigan State. Here was Wisconsin, with a 1–9 record and about to become 1–10, still working like crazy with players who were buying in to the Alvarez Way. Near the end of a midweek practice, McCarney was running sprints with Don Davey. For a team that was about to finish a winless conference season, the enthusiasm at that practice was amazing. On paper, they had no business even being on the field with the Spartans, but had it not been for a dropped pass in the end zone, the Badgers might have pulled off a stunning upset. As it turned out, Wisconsin lost 14–9, but there were signs that Alvarez and his staff had established a foundation.

Finally, there was some light at the end of a very dark tunnel.

The postseason banquet featured optimism that people had not seen in several years. Remember this is a program that had to deal with the tragic loss of Coach Dave McClain, followed by a tough year under interim coach Jim Hilles, who had the unenviable task of trying to hold things together. From there, it was three years under Don Morton, a period Badger fans just wanted to forget. In the first year under Barry Alvarez, there were signs that better days were ahead. That 1990 team won just a single game, but the Badgers were starting to win back some fans.

The process would prove to be excruciatingly painful at times, but along the way there were some memorable days, and the Badgers were just two seasons away from achieving the seemingly impossible. The fun was just beginning.

5

The '94 Rose Bowl

BARRY ALVAREZ LOVES TO SAY ALL BOWLS ARE GOOD, but he also will tell you the Rose Bowl is simply on another level. I could not agree more. Television can only show you so much. In that stadium, the grass seems to be a little bit greener, and the sky is a sharper shade of blue.

Before Barry led that 1993 team to Pasadena, the last Wisconsin squad to play in the Rose Bowl was the 1962 team. Coach Milt Bruhn led the Badgers to an 8–1 regular season record and a No. 2 ranking. The quarterback was Ron Vander Kelen. One of his favorite targets was Pat Richter, who went on to be a first-round draft pick of the Washington Redskins in 1963. Of course, Pat then went on to do a few other things in his professional career.

That 1963 Rose Bowl remains one of the most talked about bowl games of all time. Trailing 42–14 in the fourth quarter, Wisconsin nearly pulled off the mother of all comebacks with Vander Kelen, who earned MVP honors, throwing for 401 yards. Richter caught 11 passes for 163 yards. The Badgers fell five points short, but as Pat would tell you even today, the way people talk about that game, you would have thought Wisconsin actually won it.

Fans old enough to remember the game have told me they figured the Badgers would soon return to the Rose Bowl. Then the dry spell hit. Wisconsin would go bowl-less until the 1981 Garden

31

State Bowl. The following year the Badgers earned a trip to the Independence Bowl, where they won a postseason game for the first time in school history, beating Kansas State 14–3. Two years later, Wisconsin fell to Kentucky in the Hall of Fame Bowl.

Then the bowl trips stopped. As the program faded in the late 1980s, those fans who watched the Badgers in the 1963 Rose Bowl had reason to doubt whether they would live to see another trip to Southern California to ring in the New Year.

At the beginning of the 1993 season, fans were just hoping to go somewhere, anywhere. The 1992 season ended in heartbreaking fashion. With a trip to the Freedom Bowl in Anaheim at stake, the Badgers let a big one get away. On a day when they made numerous mistakes, they still had a chance to steal a victory, but in the final minute Northwestern's defense forced a fumble by running back Jason Burns, and the Wildcats escaped with a 27–25 win.

I was on the field during those last minutes, standing next to sports information director Steve Malchow. The Badgers were driving and getting into position for a field goal when the Cats' defense made a huge play. Nobody needed to say anything. One look at anyone associated with UW athletics said it all.

Many had thought the Badgers were in line for a trip to Shreveport, Louisiana, and the Independence Bowl, but Pat Richter also was talking with the Freedom Bowl folks. On the Monday after the game, I was sitting in the office of one of the administrators, who showed me a very nice pamphlet from Anaheim. The bowl was looking for a 30th anniversary "rematch" of the famous 1963 Rose Bowl between Wisconsin and USC. It was all coming together, but the Badgers fell just short of getting that sixth victory and bowl eligibility.

Within days of that gut-wrencher, defensive lineman Lamark Shackerford set the tone for the magical 1993 season. He did so during, of all things, the annual postseason banquet. I remember he told the audience that he was *really* looking forward to playing Northwestern again, as the Wildcats would have to play in Madison next year. What I thought might be a downer of a banquet turned into an upbeat evening with a team already full of resolve.

I always love the Joe Panos story of that season. When the Badgers won their Big Ten opener at Indiana, a reporter asked Joe whether Wisconsin could really be a player in the conference race. Panos' answer of, "Why not Wisconsin?" has become one of the more famous lines ever uttered by a Badger football player. Of all the great captains during the Alvarez era, Barry probably loved Joe the most, and it is a great story. When you combine the thoughts of Shackerford and Panos, one could sense the Badger football team was setting a high bar in 1993.

Shack was right, too. A week after defeating Indiana, the Badgers got their payback, drilling Northwestern 53–14.

Wisconsin moved up to 15th in the AP poll when it played Minnesota at the Metrodome. It was October 23, and as the annual rivalry game with the Gophers was going on, we got word that the Toronto Blue Jays had beaten the Philadelphia Phillies in the World Series thanks to a three-run homer in the bottom of the ninth inning from Joe Carter.

That is pretty good drama. And while a title was not at stake, there was good theatre going on in the dome. Darrell Bevell threw for a UW-record 423 yards, but turnovers helped the Gophers give the Badgers their only loss of the season.

After the game, some fans started to wonder whether the season would fall apart. Michigan was next on the schedule, and during a commercial break on Barry's radio show, I told him I had the feeling that folks were jumping off the bandwagon. All he said was, "We'll see."

He felt very good about that 1993 team and with good reason. His plan on how to build a program was coming together faster than most thought possible. Running back Brent Moss was on his way to being the Big Ten's Most Valuable Player. Panos and his fellow offensive linemen were pounding away at opposing defenses. The Wisconsin defense would give up yards, but it had a knack for making big plays, finishing the season with a plus-14 turnover margin.

The Badgers beat Michigan 13–10, but after the game I had to switch from being a sports reporter to being a news reporter. In those days, postgame player interviews were done in the McClain Center weight room. As you might imagine, the players were in a great mood and happily answered questions from the assembled media. It was quite a day. One week after a disheartening loss to Minnesota, the Badgers were right back in the title chase with a thrilling victory against the Wolverines.

In the middle of the interviews, strength and conditioning coach John Dettmann entered the room and told a few of us that it was getting ugly outside. I had no idea what he was talking about.

Soon enough, all of us in the interview room saw exactly what Dettmann meant. When I walked back into the stadium, my jaw dropped. The students tried to rush the field, but many ended up being pressed against the railing. Public address announcer Jack Rane used the dreaded words "pulse-less non-breathers," and he continued to plead for people to move away and allow the emergency workers to get to the injured fans.

Panos and some of his teammates were pulling fellow students out of the pile of humanity. Walk-on receiver Mike Brin became a household name for his efforts in saving two fans. It was a scary, surreal scene. While there were injuries, luckily there were no fatalities. As the incident was unfolding, many of us thought the ending would be far worse.

To this day, I get nervous when fans rush the field. After the Badgers beat No. 1 Ohio State in 2010, Mike Lucas and I watched with great concern when it appeared there was going to be a repeat of the 1993 Michigan game. For a few anxious moments, students again were being pinned to the railing. Thankfully, security personnel quickly took care of what could have been a real mess.

The players and coaches dealt with the near-tragedy of the 1993 postgame scene at Camp Randall, and the following week Wisconsin tied Ohio State 14–14. The Badgers were in position to win it, but OSU's Marlon Kerner blocked a potential game-winning field goal from Rick Schnetzky.

As I waited to do my postgame interview with Barry, I remember talking to a few folks who feared the Rose Bowl dream was fading. Wisconsin needed Ohio State to lose at Michigan, while the Badgers still had to win at Illinois, then go to Tokyo and beat Michigan State.

It all fell into place. The Wolverines throttled the Buckeyes, and the Badgers did the same to the Illini and the Spartans. Those fans who attended the 1963 Rose Bowl finally had a chance to return. Of course, for many, it would be their first trip to Pasadena to see their favorite team, and as the saying goes, there is no time like the first time.

The Rose Bowl was UCLA's home field, but it was that 1994 game when the term "Camp Randall West" was born. More than 70,000 Wisconsin fans made their way into the stadium with thousands more outside the Rose Bowl thanks to a ticket scam that left many out in the cold—or rather out in the parking lot.

Remember, I was not the football play-by-play announcer that year. During the game, I bounced between the radio booth and my seat alongside the newspaper writers and other broadcast media.

There is a longtime rule about no cheering in the press box, but there was one moment when many of us nearly broke it—not so much by cheering, but rather by letting out a big "oohhhhhh." It was when quarterback Darrell Bevell, not exactly known for his nimble feet, ran for a 21-yard fourth-quarter touchdown. He put a nifty little juke move on a UCLA defensive player. With all due respect to the great running backs in Wisconsin history, to me Bevell's play is the greatest run in Badgers' history. Many of us in the press box struggled to contain ourselves. I do not believe anyone was being a cheerleader—we just understood that long runs were not exactly a huge part of Darrell Bevell's skill set. I can only imagine what fans watching back home were yelling.

This Rose Bowl, like so many before and since, came down to the final minute. With the Bruins out of timeouts, quarterback Wayne Cook faced some pressure from the Badgers defense. He then made the ill-fated decision to run the ball.

After the game, I asked defensive lineman Mike Thompson what happened. "I rushed outside," he stated. "He [Cook] cut back inside of me. I came off the block and made the play and just laid on him. He was trying to get up, and I was just kind of hanging on to let the clock run down."

The clock did run down. As time expired, announcer Brian Manthey shouted, "Thank you Wayne Cook!" A few seconds later, Manthey perfectly described the historic moment. "The greatest game in Wisconsin history is no longer a loss. It's a victory on the turf in the Rose Bowl." He was referring to the 1963 Rose Bowl, which many did consider to be the Badgers' greatest game. It remains a great game, but on January 1, 1994, there was a new No. 1.

During those closing minutes, I was down on the field near the Wisconsin bench. When the clock struck zero, I really thought for a moment that we were having an earthquake. I am serious. The Badgers fans were going crazy, and the players on the bench were up for grabs. Fans were crying. Players were laughing and crying. It was the most remarkable scene I had ever witnessed in person.

Some of the players were doing interviews on the field, and a few of us gathered around center Cory Raymer, who told us how he ripped into a UCLA player for allowing Bevell to fake him out of his jock. Free safety Scott Nelson was explaining to reporters that he had proposed to his girlfriend Becky on the field, and she said yes. When I heard that story, all I could think of was "Are you kidding me?" What movie producer wouldn't go for this script?

The locker room was a mob scene. I was in there interviewing Barry for our radio network. "I'm just floatin' right now," was his first answer to whatever it was I asked.

He too loved his quarterback's dash to the end zone. "Ol' Bev looked like one of those old Oklahoma quarterbacks whistling down the field!"

It was classic Alvarez, who knew just the right buttons to push. Turns out UCLA helped push a few of those buttons. Before the game, there was a little chirping going on. "They [UCLA] came out and were bad-mouthing our kids, they were trash talking our kids," he said. "I love it when that happens—we can feed on that. I'll tell you something. Nobody is gonna intimidate this crew! Now, they may beat us, and they may run past us and all that stuff, but they are *not* going to intimidate our guys. That motivates them."

He was so right. Running back Terrell Fletcher added, "They went out of their way to come into our drills. There is no reason for that, man. They come into our drill and just start critiquing us, talking noise. So we're like, 'Man, why don't you just get the hell out of here!'"

That was the 1993 team in a nutshell. It was a no-nonsense group that thrived on being doubted. Barry's best teams did a great job of embracing that mentality. The '98 team was supposed to be the worst team to ever play in the Rose Bowl. If you are Alvarez, that is a perfect setup. The '99 team was headed downhill after losing to Cincinnati and Michigan. That was just the fuel Barry and his team could use to their advantage.

Why not Wisconsin, indeed.

6

Stu and Stan

IN MY HUMBLE OPINION, one of the University of Wisconsin's more underappreciated basketball coaches is Stu Jackson. When his name popped up as a strong candidate to replace Steve Yoder, many people were caught by surprise. Names that were swirling around town included Ben Braun, who is a UW graduate and at the time was the head coach at Eastern Michigan. Other possibilities, as described in *Always a Badger: The Pat Richter Story*, written by Vince Sweeney, included Mike Brey, Jim Cleamons, Tony Barone, Dick Bennett, Bo Ryan, and a Michigan State assistant coach named Tom Izzo. The book relates a great line from Spartans head coach Jud Heathcote, who saw Richter and Izzo talking the morning of a Michigan State–Northwestern game in Evanston. Sweeney relays the quote from Jud, "Hey Tom, did he tell you he's cutting basketball?"

By his own admission, Richter knew little about Jackson, the former New York Knicks coach who, after being fired, went on to become the NBA's assistant vice president of operations. Make no mistake, Jackson's name meant something to many in the basketball world, which I believe Richter realized fairly quickly. A former assistant under Rick Pitino at Providence College as well as the Knicks, Stu Jackson was considered a real coup for the University of Wisconsin.

In his opening news conference at the Field House, Jackson was very clear on what he wanted to do with the Badgers. "When teams

39

play Wisconsin, we want them to know that they are in for a game."
Adding, "There is no reason why Wisconsin can't be on par with any
program in America."

In his two seasons in Madison, Stu certainly rubbed some people the wrong way. He had a presence, and he could be intimidating
if you allowed him to be. Jackson also had a pretty quick temper. Yet
similar to Barry Alvarez, Jackson was just what the doctor ordered.
If he thought something needed to be said, or something needed to
change at the UW, he did not really care if his blunt remarks hurt
anybody's feelings.

He knew the Field House was worn down. "Can we at least
give it a coat of paint?" he asked. He once griped that the Badgers
lost a game because the barn was just too damn cold. Jackson
also caused a bit of a stir when he wanted to replace the center court logo. At the time, the Bucky Badger insignia graced the
mid-stripe. Jackson wanted to do anything he could to give the
Badgers a national identity. Stu thought if you were unfamiliar
with certain mascots, what good is it for somebody watching on
TV from the East Coast to see Bucky at center court? It was a
good question, so he ordered the block W. The motion W started
with Barry and the football team, then it eventually made its way
to the other sports.

Jackson also wanted to refer to his program as Wisconsin
Basketball, not Badger Basketball. It was the same reasoning as the
mascot logo—he wanted to get the Wisconsin name out there as
much as he could. Maybe this sounds really simple, and believe me,
some people complained about losing good old Bucky from the
Field House floor, but that was the state of Wisconsin basketball in
the early 1990s. The teams were getting better, and the crowds were
getting bigger, but the Badgers were still fighting a very uphill battle
to get on the national stage.

Stu's first game as the Badgers coach was less than ideal.
Wisconsin opened at the old Rosemont Horizon against Loyola, and

the Ramblers won on a last-second basket. After wins against Dick Bennett's UW–Green Bay team, and a romp of Bethune-Cookman, the Badgers lost for the first and, as of this writing, the only time in series history to UW–Milwaukee. I remember thinking before the game that this had the potential to be ugly. The Panthers, under head coach Steve Antrim, had a very good team that year with players such as Craig Green and Marc Mitchell. I just thought it had the makings of a bad matchup for Wisconsin.

Frankly, I thought the Badgers did rather well to lose by just five points. However, a 77–72 home loss to what many considered a so-called "mid-major" in-state school did not go over well with the Badger fan base. Stu was livid, and you are correct in assuming practices following that game were not a lot of fun.

Stu never seemed to worry much about making friends among fellow conference coaches. Following a loss to Purdue, he drew the ire of Boilermaker's coach Gene Keady. Glenn Robinson had just put on a typically outstanding performance, and during the post-game media session, Jackson suggested that the Big Dog was NBA ready "right now." Keady did not appreciate what he thought was an attempt by another coach to convince Robinson to go pro.

Stu was right. In the rematch on February 13, 1993, Robinson and Badger sophomore Michael Finley staged a duel that turned out to be one of the better games at the Field House in recent memory. Finley dropped 33 points on the Boilers. Unfortunately, Robinson poured in 42, and Purdue prevailed in a 90–87 double-overtime thriller. Wisconsin was in position to win a couple of times, including in the final minute of regulation when the Badgers led by five points. But a Matt Waddell three-pointer, followed by a Robinson layup, sent the game into OT. By the second overtime, Boilermaker Matt Painter knocked down a pair of big free throws to help Purdue seal the game.

One of the better episodes I heard involving Stu came after that game. As the story goes, the locker room was very quiet and somber after such a tough loss. However, players do expend a lot of energy, and being young men between the ages of 18 and 22, they were hungry. In the room were a few boxes of soft pretzels, just something to tide them over until they left the gym and got something more to eat. However, these players were not stupid. They knew the head coach was going to come in and talk to the team, and no one dared be seen eating when a coach in a lousy mood entered the room.

So, as I am told, the room was still dead quiet. Enter Stu Jackson for a postgame chewing-out after the team let what would have been a terrific victory slip away. He finished his talk and exited the locker room—or so the players thought. They waited for a little bit, just to make certain Stu was gone for good. Believing that was the case, one of the players decided it was safe to dive into the pretzels. Lo and behold, here comes Stu for one or two more parting shots. The guilty player stopped eating, but he was caught. Stu was smoking mad—again, wondering how anyone can be hungry after a gut-wrenching loss. Finally, Stu decided, "Here, go ahead—have another pretzel," and fired a fastball across the room. Instead of ducking for cover, the player smoothly reached out and snatched the thrown pretzel, much like a first baseman would snag a bullet throw from third, and downed a second helping of the postgame snack. Yes, it was a bitter defeat, but when you are hungry, you are hungry, right?

Since the locker room is closed to the media during that period, I can only rely on what I heard. Others in the room confirmed it. Whatever the case, it is a pretty good story, and I am sticking to it.

Stu's first Wisconsin team made the NIT but fell in the first round to Rice. Expectations were higher for year two, in large part because of a recruiting class that had Badgers fans counting down the days to the first game and buying tickets at a rate not seen in a very long time.

Even prior to Jackson arriving in Madison, assistant coach Ray McCallum had been recruiting a 7' center from Chicago's King High School. Rashard Griffith was coveted by many, but it appeared to be little more than a pipe dream that the big man would choose Wisconsin. When Stu arrived, the recruiting process intensified. I always will remember the fairly frequent phone conversations I had with David Kaplan, who is now a very talented sports talk host at WGN Radio in Chicago as well as the host of the *Chicago Tribune Live* TV show. I suppose you could call Kaplan a basketball lifer, having coached at Northern Illinois and scouting for a couple of NBA teams. In the early 1990s, among the many hats Kap wore was that of a Chicago-area high school hoops expert. Kaplan led me to believe that the Badgers had a real shot of landing this star, and sure enough, they did.

Also in that recruiting class was Jalil Roberts, who played for Bob Hurley's famed program in Jersey City, New Jersey, and Darnell Hoskins, a gifted guard from Dayton, Ohio. But it was Griffith who stole the show, and it was Griffith who led to a sharp increase in ticket sales. Players out of Chicago with his size and resume tend to choose schools other than Wisconsin. While some wondered exactly how the Badgers landed such a prized recruit, others such as myself wondered how long of a delay there would be if and when he shattered a backboard.

In 1988, the University of Pittsburgh's Jerome Lane did just that. The assist on the window-breaking jam came from Panthers guard Sean Miller, who was an assistant under Stu in the 1992–93 season. Knowing it had already happened just a few years ago, it made perfect sense that Griffith might bust a backboard at the Field House. For the record, it never happened, but if it would have, school officials told me back then that they would have needed 30 minutes to get a new board in place.

The 1993–94 team, with its celebrated freshman class along with outstanding guard Tracy Webster and emerging star Michael Finley, ran off eleven straight wins to start the season. The Badgers got some payback on UW–Milwaukee, trouncing the Panthers in the season opener 106–84.

Game two was notable not because the Badgers traveled to Los Angeles and drilled Loyola Marymount 103–67. It was notable because the game took place on the same night the Badger football team beat Michigan State in Tokyo to clinch the school's first Rose Bowl berth in 31 years. LMU's home gym was pretty small, but the crowd was good, thanks to several hundred Badgers fans taking advantage of a rare opportunity to see their team on the West Coast. The atmosphere was pretty good—for about one half. With the Badgers in control of the game, and with kickoff from Tokyo approaching, UW fans starting pouring out of the gym. Actually, it was kind of like a fire drill. With Barry's boys on the brink of making history, there was no way long-suffering UW football fans were going to miss the game with the Spartans.

Our broadcast position was right by the Wisconsin bench. I was wondering whether Stu was going to erupt again, but he understood. In fact, with his team cruising along in the second half, I would get updates on what was going on with the football game and would jot down the score and slip the piece of paper Stu's way. He also wanted to know how things were going on the other side of the world.

After the basketball game, we raced back to the hotel to catch the rest of the football game. Pat Stiegman, who back then was working for the *Milwaukee Journal-Sentinel* (these days he is a big shot at ESPN. com, but he's still a good guy), joined me as we made our way to a suite where assistant coaches Stan Van Gundy, Bob Beyer, and Tim Buckley were watching the fourth quarter. After the Badgers clinched the Big Ten title, Stiegman and I decided we needed to visit a little place called the Baja Cantina, a joint full of beautiful people who could not have cared less about the Badgers sealing a bid to Pasadena. Pat and I did care, and we thought it was appropriate to raise a glass or two. Or maybe even three. Isn't it amazing how you can always remember where you were and what you were doing when a big event unfolds?

Now, back to basketball, and after that red-hot 11–0 start, the Badgers did not win consecutive games the rest of the way.

Although the Big Ten had no teams in the Final Four, the league was very good. As for the Badgers, they stumbled down the stretch, losing six of their final eight games. Some fans were concerned, and some in the media were quite skeptical about the Badgers' chances of making the NCAA field. But the body of work was plenty good enough, and for the first time since 1947, Wisconsin was in the tournament.

The ninth-seeded Badgers were shipped to Ogden, Utah, for a first-round game against eighth-seeded Cincinnati. Even as a broadcaster, I remember how nervous I felt before that game. Bob Huggins had a solid team, featuring Damon Flint and Dontonio Wingfield. The game was tight most of the way, with Cincinnati holding a one-point lead with ten minutes to play. Then Wisconsin broke out on a 22–12 run with Griffith, a very average-at-best free throw shooter, knocking down 12-of-14 from the line. The Badgers also got valuable minutes from Darnell Hoskins, but Finley and Griffith did the most damage, each scoring 22 points. Rashard also added 15 rebounds. After the game the guys were fired up. Forward Brian Kelley came over our table and wanted the microphone for a few seconds to say hello to everyone back home.

The victory certainly helped put to rest any doubts whether or not the Badgers were NCAA worthy. It also set up an interesting second-round match-up with the West Region's top seed, Missouri. Given the often lower-scoring games of recent years, younger fans are some-times surprised to know that the 1994 game against Missouri was a true shootout, with the Tigers winning 109–96. Once again, Finley was outstanding, pouring in 36 points, and Tracy Webster's final game as a Badger was excellent as well, adding 27 points and dishing out seven assists. The bad news was Griffith was limited by foul trouble. He played just 16 minutes. Couple that with the fact that Wisconsin had no answer for Big Eight Player of the Year Melvin Booker, who scored 35 that day, and the Badgers' season came to an end.

Also ending that summer was Stu's run as Wisconsin's coach. A friend of his once told me that he figured Stu left the New York

Knicks with a bad taste in his mouth, and if the opportunity to run an NBA team came along, he likely would jump at the chance. That opportunity presented itself with the expansion Vancouver Grizzlies, which hired Jackson as its first general manager.

I will never blame him for leaving, but the timing of Jackson's departure put Pat Richter in a tough spot. By July, that left little if any time to conduct a thorough coaching search, but it appeared Richter had a pretty good answer to his coaching question already on staff. The players, including Griffith, seemed strongly in favor of elevating Stan Van Gundy. "Stan's the man," Rashard said. Despite some concerns about Van Gundy's lack of head-coaching experience, Jackson's top assistant moved over one chair.

Simply put, Stan Van Gundy is a beauty, and I really enjoyed working with him. The Stan Van Gundy that fans saw at Wisconsin, and the one fans watched with the Orlando Magic, is not necessarily the Van Gundy I got to know.

I believe Van Gundy never had the sense that he was exactly the "people's choice" for the Badgers gig. Perhaps he was right, but I also think that team was not nearly as good as advertised. Some preseason publications had the Badgers as Top 10 material, but I always thought the loss of Webster was underestimated. Hoskins was a nice player, but for my money Webster was not just a standout player, he was the glue, and they dearly missed his leadership.

The first real sign of trouble came on December 10, 1994, in Ypsilanti, Michigan. The Badgers won their first four games, but going into the Eastern Michigan game, Griffith was nursing a tender foot. He did not play that night, and the game turned into a disaster. Eleven minutes into the first half, the Badgers trailed 32–4. That is not a misprint. It was 32–4. At the half, the score was 50–17.

Van Gundy and everyone else connected to the Wisconsin program looked stunned. The only thing that saved the game from being an absolute trip to the woodshed was Michael Finley's scoring spree. He ended up tying a single-game UW record with 42 points, but even his effort was not close to being enough. No other Badger scored more than eight points. They were guilty of 21 turnovers. Eastern won 92–76. The next day at a Badger football bowl practice, assistant coach Jim Hueber told me, "I was listening to the game, and when I heard you give the score, I thought you just made a mistake." I wish it was a mistake.

The season had very few highlights, an exception being on January 14 at home against Minnesota when Finley broke Danny Jones' career scoring record. But any momentum would not last. After winning three straight in early February, the Badgers dropped six of their final seven games. They closed the season at Michigan State on a day when the Spartans honored retiring coach Jud Heathcote.

By then Stan knew his fate but kept it from his team. I remember doing an interview with Tom Izzo, who was set to follow Heathcote as the Spartans head coach. He seemed to be well aware that there was going to be another change in Madison, with Dick Bennett's name already on the radar.

The game offered up quite the contrast. Michigan State won going away. Shawn Respert kissed the floor, and Jud's final regular season game was a rousing success. Meanwhile, official Ed Hightower did the Badgers a little favor. Frustration was reaching a breaking point, and one of the players was struggling to keep his emotions in check. A good official understands what can happen in the heat of the moment, especially with a good player whose team is having a disappointing season. Hightower went to the Badgers bench and suggested that while he didn't want to eject anyone, it might be a good idea to take him out of the game. Stan did, and the Badgers went on to a very dispirited performance, losing 97–72. It was a tough way to end the season, and an unfortunate ending for a senior class that had a good supply of talent led by Finley, who to me is on the short list of the greatest players to wear a Wisconsin basketball uniform.

I will tell anyone who is willing to listen that Stan Van Gundy is a very smart basketball man, and he is an even better person. A true basketball junkie, he also has interests in other things. We would talk about books, especially John Grisham novels. We would laugh about certain local TV shows, including something on Madison's local cable-access channel called *Three Guys Talk Hockey*. It was a hoot—three dudes wearing hockey jerseys talking all things NHL. Stan also loves baseball. When Stan was an assistant with the Miami Heat, he was a regular at Florida Marlins games, even serving as a "correspondent" during the playoffs for ESPN's short-lived *Cold Pizza* show.

His agent is Tim Valentyn, who also represents Bo Ryan. A few years ago former basketball athletic trainer Andy Winterstein and I visited Tim in his downtown Madison office, and we placed a conference call to Van Gundy. It was a fun chat, even though Stan gave me grief for the many live-commercial reads I do during a basketball broadcast. I guess he caught part of a broadcast one night. "Hey Matt, love your work, especially those corn grower ads you read." Stan is such a city boy.

It is too bad most folks do not get to see that side of Stan. Then again, he is who he is, and I have my doubts whether he really cares what most people think. He strikes me as someone who fully understands the nature of big-time sports, and the good and the bad that can go with it. We haven't hooked up in a few years, but Tim tells me that Stan hasn't changed a bit, which I think is a very good thing.

I think it is also fair to say that Stan learned some valuable lessons in his year as Wisconsin's head coach, and while he has had his clashes with players at the NBA level, the record shows that he is a heck of a coach.

Given the success of Wisconsin athletics the last several years, it might be easy to brush aside the contributions of Stu Jackson and Stan Van Gundy, but it would be misguided to dismiss their value. They were in town for a brief period of time, but they certainly aided in the growth of Wisconsin basketball.

7

Four Personalities, Same Core Values

SOME OF THE MORE FREQUENTLY ASKED QUESTIONS fans will ask is, "What is coach so-and-so really like? Is so-and-so always that angry?" You get the idea. With the Badgers' success, not to mention the fact that nearly every football and basketball game is available on TV, fans have the chance to view a coach in his best and worst on-the-job moments.

It only makes sense for you to wonder what makes them tick. What is interesting to me is in the last 15 years of Wisconsin football and basketball, the four coaches to reach a high level of success are quite different from one another in some ways, yet each seems to share a very similar philosophy on how to build a team. None attended the University of Wisconsin. However, three of these coaches are a lock to be forever linked to the rise of Badger athletics, and a fourth appears to be well on his way.

In case you haven't yet figured it out, those four men are Barry Alvarez, Bret Bielema, Dick Bennett, and Bo Ryan. These four coaches have distinctly different personalities, but they all have proven to be the right fit at the right school at the right time.

There are those who refer to Alvarez as the Godfather. I am not sure how many people say that to his face, but it is a nickname that is sometimes attached to this College Football Hall of Fame coach.

He does have that look, doesn't he? The nearly year-round tan, the nice threads, and that look of confidence are hard not to notice. That line from his opening news conference "You had better get your season tickets now, because before long, you won't be able to" shows a fair amount of confidence.

Barry Alvarez is one of those rare human beings who can command attention the moment he enters a room. For me, this is especially noticeable when we are at an event in Wisconsin but outside of Madison. Don't get me wrong, he still turns plenty of heads in town, but it is even more obvious at a function in Milwaukee, Green Bay, Monroe, Wisconsin Dells, or any other town. People tend to stop what they are doing and just look. Occasionally, a Badger fan will show no fear and approach Barry right away, but often people just keep their distance and whisper, "Hey, look who is here. It's Coach Alvarez!"

Of all the people I have had a chance to know while covering sports, I would have to say nobody enjoys being who he is more than Barry Alvarez. I say that as a compliment. "I have fun every day," he has said. When he arrived in 1990, he and his assistants hit the ground running. He was used to winning, as a player at Nebraska; as a high school coach in Mason City, Iowa; as an assistant at Iowa; and as an assistant at Notre Dame. He had a plan on how to win at Wisconsin, and he went about executing that plan, and the hell with anyone who got in his way. It was just what was needed for a badly ailing football program.

It is difficult for a coach to last at one school longer than 8–10 years. Just my opinion, but I believe the key for Barry lasting 16 years as the Badgers head coach was his ability to enjoy success. In the coaching world, that does not always happen. Pat Riley, a championship NBA coach with the Los Angeles Lakers and the Miami Heat, has said, "There is winning, and there is misery." Legendary football coach Bill Parcells said he would start thinking about the next game as he was walking off the field on Sunday, and win or lose, he generally would be in a lousy mood on Mondays.

Barry is cut a bit differently. He often said, "It is hard to win." So when the Badgers won, be it against Ohio State or Murray State, Wisconsin's ball coach allowed himself some time to feel good about it. We taped his TV shows on Sunday mornings because he wanted to get home after a game as soon as he could. Generally, there would be a house full of family, friends, and other supporters, and if the Badgers won that day, he wanted to get home ASAP, watch the other games, and celebrate the victory. Of course, if the game did not go so well, Barry admitted he sometimes would just head up to his room, but after he got the program going, the Badgers tended to win more than they lost.

It is fun to watch him now as the school's athletics director. It is much the same, only now his excitement is for any sport on campus that has a signature win. The man gets so fired up after a big victory that he will high-five and give a big hug to any number of people. After all, he knows winning is hard, and when you do win, enjoy it. Give yourself a little time before you start worrying about the next game.

◆ ◆ ◆

Then there is Dick Bennett. Of the four coaches, Alvarez and Bennett would appear to most as being the least similar. Maybe part of it is because basketball coaches tend to get more "face time" on TV during games. Many fans wondered and worried about Bennett's health, fearing he might suffer a stroke while yelling at a player or an official.

To be honest, I worried, too. He would get so worked up that many of us in the media who attended practice on a regular basis wondered whether he would collapse on the court, as has happened to other coaches. While not every player liked Bennett's methods, most guys understood how to take him. If nothing else, they knew that if he went on a rant, it meant they had a little break during practice.

If the Badgers were preparing for a team that liked to use a zone, Bennett would put his team through a "zone game" in practice, which could mean they would be playing five-on-seven, as in five offensive players against seven defensive players. Yes, there were many days when baskets were few and far between. I started to cringe when they would get to that point in a practice, and if I started to cringe, imagine how some of the players must have felt. Missed shots, turnovers, and a tongue lashing were just around the corner.

I never thought he pushed his religious beliefs, but Bennett's teams knew about the head coach's strong faith. That is what sometimes made his outbursts a little humorous. A fact of life in sports is that the language can get pretty salty. That is not breaking news, and I am not going to go into vivid detail about what is said during a practice. I will make one minor exception here. There would be that rare occasion during a practice, probably during a zone game, where Dick would get so angry that he would clench his fists, hesitate for a few seconds, then finally let fly with a yell of "Dammit!" There were times when a couple of players *really* struggled to keep from laughing.

Yet off the court, I have not met a gentler human being. I don't know how many times we would talk, and Dick would say, "Well Matt, I apologized to [Mark] Vershaw today," or someone else. Then he would beat himself up for being so tough on his players. We would talk about so many things, especially after our pregame radio interview, which he liked to do after the shoot around when possible. We would chat about golf, family, books, and probably more golf. The man is obsessed with golf. He is a regular at a local golf shop called Nevada Bob's, where he is constantly trying out new clubs. His son, Tony, once said, "If you ever want to get into my dad's head, just wait 'til he pulls out his driver and then tell him that you heard some bad things about that club. That usually messes him up."

Dick was unusually accommodating with the media, and while not everyone liked how his teams played, writers and broadcasters enjoyed covering his news conferences. He can appear to be shy in a crowd, but he is quite the public speaker. I am not sure how much he still does "Casey at the Bat," but those who have heard Bennett give his rendition say it is top notch.

He also likes to make fun of himself. He would talk to groups and say, "You know, if you think about it, I could teach Barry's teams how to pass, and his teams could show us how to run." Bennett knew there were critics of his team's style, and perhaps that made the Final Four run that much sweeter. I know it did for me. Dick has been, and always will be a dear friend, and it is fun when we get the chance to visit, and of course, play a little golf.

• • •

While Bennett sometimes can appear to be shy, Bo Ryan can work a room with the best of them. Before she coached her first game, new women's basketball coach Bobbie Kelsey had a great line about Bo. "You know how some people can drink you under the table?" she said with a smirk, "Bo Ryan can talk you under the table." A few of us wanted to name Bobbie the Big Ten Coach of the Year right away.

Bo has a great knack for interacting with people of all ages and backgrounds. No doubt that goes back to his days in his beloved hometown of Chester, Pennsylvania, just outside of Philadelphia. He loves to talk about being a point guard, a shortstop, and a quarterback. I always look forward to trips to Penn State because it turns into a reunion with many of his old Wilkes College teammates. The man has not forgotten where he came from, and if he ever did, his buddies Herb Kemp and Jay Holliday would straighten him out in a hurry.

The loyalty former players and other supporters show for Bo is impressive. It is amazing how many Platteville Pioneers fans have become diehard Wisconsin Badger fans, gobbling up their fair share of season tickets. Several will even drive to Madison for Bo's Monday night radio show. Before I ever got to know him, many of Ryan's friends would tell me how he would be a great coach at Wisconsin. I have to admit I really did not know how it would work out, which is another reason why I will never accuse myself of being very smart.

Bo will always fight for what he believes is right. In 2008, the Badgers were sent on the road for the Big Ten/ACC Challenge for the third time in four years. The head coach was more than a little upset about it, and he stated his case to anyone willing to listen. He fought for and won the opportunity for the Badgers to host the next two years of the Challenge, with Duke coming to town in 2009 and North Carolina State making the trip to Madison in 2010.

He also fought to have an academic center located in the same building where the team plays its games, practices, and gets treatments. As a result, there is the Kohl Fetzer Center. The KFC, as it is called, also has been helpful to women's basketball and both the men's and women's hockey teams, among others.

Maybe you are aware that in a news conference Bo Ryan has a tendency to ramble. I guess that is like saying it gets kind of cold in Wisconsin during the winter. It can get funny at times. Ask him about the progress of a particular player, and Bo will respond with a story about how he and his father, Butch, snuck into Franklin Field to watch the 1960 NFL Championship Game between the Philadelphia Eagles and the Green Bay Packers.

Yet when it comes to the most important part of the job, coaching, Bo Ryan gets to the point. For almost his entire life, Paul Chryst has known Bo. Paul's father, the late George Chryst, hired Bo at Platteville. A couple of years ago Paul attended a practice, and Bo invited him to sit in on a team video session. Paul told me how straight to the point Bo was with his players. No B.S., no stories with ten different tangents. Chryst said it was just a good old-fashioned classroom session.

Bo Ryan's ability to get his players to improve each year is uncanny. That might sound simple, but take a look across the country. Certainly there are some terrific coaches in college basketball, but I have my doubts whether there are many programs where players so consistently improve their games.

If the biggest fault people have with Bo Ryan is that he can be a difficult interview, I think the Wisconsin Badgers and their fans will survive the blow.

• • •

Finally, there is Bret Bielema. While Bo Ryan grew up next door to the big city, Bret lived on a hog farm in Prophetstown, Illinois. Among the skills he learned was how to be an auctioneer. Trust me, he is pretty good.

Bielema is the first coach I have worked with who is several years younger than yours truly (eight to be exact), and maybe in part because of that I feel comfortable giving him grief from time to time. We hit it off fairly quickly through a mutual friend, long-time Iowa broadcaster Gary Dolphin, who obviously got to know Bielema during his days with the Hawkeyes. When the coach and I go back and forth, a typical exchange could be Bret saying, "You know, I really think Dolph would be a great Voice of the Badgers." And I will respond, "Sounds good to me. I always wanted to work with Kirk Ferentz."

I think sometimes people get the wrong impression of Bielema. To some, he can appear to be pretty cocky. Certainly there are things he has said during or after games that he would like to have back, but who wouldn't? A perk of jobs like mine is that we can see another side of coaches, and the Bret I know is down to earth.

He is a believer in the power of the pen. In an age of texting (which he and I often do), he is old school enough to understand that a handwritten note goes a long way. The week of the Wisconsin–Ohio State game in 2010, my counterpart with the Buckeyes, Paul Keels, needed to spend a few days in the hospital and would miss the trip to Madison. Paul is one of my best friends in the business, and when I got the news, I was rattled as hell. I told Bret about it. He has met Keels, but he does not really know him well at all. Still, Bret wrote Paul a note wishing him a speedy recovery (and he did get better quickly). Believe it when I tell you that letter meant a lot to Paul Keels, and it meant a lot to me that Bret would take the time during a hectic week to do such a thing.

Another time I was sitting in Bret's office, getting ready to record an interview, when we were talking about a promising player named Justin Ostrowski, whose career was going to end because of a bad knee. Bielema loved Ostrowski, and before we started the interview, Bret was telling me about him and just started to cry. This was not about what the loss of such a player meant to the team, it was about how sorry Bret was that a player who loves the game was going to have to give it up way too early.

It has been enjoyable watching this young coach grow and establish himself as a respected figure in college football. Going into year number seven, the 42-year-old Bret Bielema is moving up the seniority chart among Big Ten coaches. Hard to believe, isn't it?

Bret might have a little more sense of adventure than the other three coaches. He certainly shows no fear in running trick plays. You just never know when that next fake punt or fake field goal is going to occur.

Like the other coaches, he enjoys a round of golf, but unlike the others, he also enjoys deep sea fishing. During a rare down time in his profession, Bret will take a trip every summer to some tropical island where electricity is lacking. He and his buddies will just rough it, catch a few fish, and no doubt have plenty of laughs.

So what do these four coaches have in common? Maybe more than you think. Take a look at how they build their teams. Do you see a lot of flash? Not really. Do you see recruiting classes that "experts" rate among the nation's best year after year? The answer is no.

What you do see is a group of coaches who will constantly emphasize fundamentals. Bret has called Wisconsin a developmental program, and perhaps that term applies to both football and basketball. Each of the four coaches stresses taking care of the ball, making smart decisions, and playing good defense. Maybe there is nothing sexy about any of that, but it is hard to argue with the results.

All four came to Wisconsin because they wanted to be here, not because the UW won some bidding war for their services. All four focus on the reasons you can win at Wisconsin, rather than griping about whatever might be holding them back. Maybe none of them is a University of Wisconsin graduate, but there can be no question each has given UW alums and all other Badger fans memories to last a lifetime.

And I believe it is safe to say all four are proud to be Badgers.

8

I Can't Believe
I'm Going to Say It

AFTER WATCHING THE FOOTBALL TEAM win back-to-back Rose Bowls and seeing Ron Dayne become the NCAA's all-time career rushing leader en route to winning the Heisman Trophy, Badger fans were riding high. Who knew there was so much more to come? While the football team may not have been everyone's pick to win Big Ten titles, most figured it had a chance to be pretty good, and there was certainly a lot of excitement about Dayne's chase to the record as well as the Heisman.

The 1999–2000 basketball team didn't quite generate that kind of anticipation. When last seen in the 1999 NCAA Tournament in Charlotte, North Carolina, the Badgers fired brick after brick in losing to Steve Alford's Southwest Missouri State team 43–32. "Will Dick Bennett's style ever work?" some fans were asking, and no doubt many had concluded the answer was no.

That 1998–99 team was actually putting together an excellent season, but by late February it appeared to be running low on fuel. After dropping its first two conference games, a four-point loss at Michigan, followed by an overtime setback to Ohio State, Wisconsin reeled off seven straight victories. That Ohio State game probably should have been postponed. It was January 2, and the Madison area was getting hit with a blizzard. My engineer, Al Skinner, and I were returning from the Rose Bowl on a red-eye flight from Los Angeles connecting through Minneapolis. I think our flight was the last plane to get into Madison before the airport was shut down. Mike Lucas and his wife, Peggy, were trying to get home via Chicago, but their own travel delays prevented them from getting back in time.

The Buckeyes arrived in Madison on New Year's Day before the weather turned for the worse. Naturally, since the team was in town, Coach Jim O'Brien wanted to play. The last thing he or any coach in his shoes would want to do is keep his team holed up in a hotel for an extra day. With most of the UW athletic administration still in Los Angeles with the football team, Dick Bennett made the decision to play the game as scheduled.

It was a terrific game. Too bad the Kohl Center was about 80 percent empty. The Badgers could have used a little more support as Michael Redd and company eked out a 78–74 victory.

With that loss behind them, the Badgers started to roll, beginning with a 66–51 thumping of 12th-ranked Michigan State. It would be the last time a Bennett-coached team beat the Spartans. Going into February, the Badgers were 7–2 and in the mix for the conference championship. Those hopes were slipping away after consecutive road defeats at Indiana and Illinois, but Wisconsin bounced back with home victories against Northwestern and Penn State.

Then the wheels started to fall off. The Badgers fell to Michigan State in East Lansing on a day when the Spartans clinched the league title. They also lost at Ohio State 63–54. Then on senior day came a hard-to-watch 51–39 loss to Michigan. The Badgers finished the regular season with a respectable 9–7 conference mark, but there was disappointment about what might have been.

In the Big Ten tournament, the Badgers' offense came alive in a 74–60 victory against Iowa. What is memorable to me is one of those precious Dick Bennett moments. Our broadcast location was right by the Wisconsin bench. At one point in the first half, a tough call went against the Badgers. It was one of those either/or calls an official has to make many times every game, and with the Badgers slumping, it just figured they would not get any breaks. Bennett was furious. He turned away from the floor and slammed his hands on the table right in front of me. On the broadcast, you can hear a little "thump" sound under my voice.

The officials either did not see it—or they decided to give him a pass—because there was no technical. A few minutes later there was a media timeout. After the team broke its huddle, I made eye contact with Bennett. He asked me whether the official made the right call. At that moment I figured if I told him the guy blew it, Dick would erupt again, which is the last thing this squad needed. So even though I really did not know for sure if it was a good or a bad call, I just said, "Dick, I think he got it right." He responded with a quick nod of his head and went back to work.

After the game, I went up to Dick and made a confession. "Hey, you know that call you were asking about? I lied." We both had a good laugh.

That might have been the final light moment of the season. In the conference semi-finals, Michigan State advanced with a 56–41 decision. From there, it was on to the nightmare in Charlotte.

It might be easy to say this now, but I believe the make-up of that team allowed it to recover from such a sour ending. Mike Kelley, Andy Kowske, Mark Vershaw, Jon Bryant, Maurice Linton, and all the rest had a way of being ultra competitive, yet this group could poke fun at itself and understood its limitations. Bennett's line, "Know who you are," keeps coming back.

While it seems almost everyone in college basketball schedules those "guarantee" games, for several years the Badgers have not been shy about giving themselves some hard non-conference tests. Bennett and Bo Ryan are believers that tough games in November and December can pay off later. That 1999–2000 schedule had two good tests right out of the gate at the NABC Classic in Syracuse,

New York. The Badgers opened by beating Missouri and then lost to the Orange. At the end of November, Wisconsin was humbled with another one of those unsightly performances, a 67–48 drilling at Wake Forest.

They started December with three straight victories, beating Rhode Island, 10th-ranked Texas, and then UW–Green Bay. The unusual part of this stretch is the Badgers had rare, non-tournament back-to-back games on December 7 and December 8 against the Longhorns and the Phoenix. The Texas game was impressive. Kelley rattled the Longhorns with 10 steals. It was a superb performance, but Kelley and his teammates knew that game would mean nothing if they laid an egg the next night against a school where Bennett once coached.

There was no reason to worry. A suffocating defense helped the Badgers put away UWGB 55–34. For Bennett, leaving Green Bay was difficult, and I don't think he enjoyed going against them. Most people around the Badgers' program also were aware that losing to the Phoenix would make matters worse.

One of the stranger broadcasting nights that season occurred during the following game on December 11 in Tampa against the University of South Florida. It was strange for a couple of reasons. First, on that Saturday night, the Heisman Trophy was going to be awarded. While it would have been a thrill to be in New York City to see Ron Dayne win the award, duty called. Besides, neither Mike nor I really like missing games.

The basketball game was close; it went down to the final minute. I told my producer that I wanted him to tell me the Heisman results as soon as the announcement was made. In the closing minute of the basketball game with the Badgers bringing the ball up the floor, we got word that Ron had won. There we were—in Tampa, watching a down-to-the-wire basketball game, and I'm telling our listening audience that the University of Wisconsin has its second-ever Heisman Trophy winner.

The Badgers lost that night 66–63, but our broadcast crew could not help but feel pretty good. Yes, the basketball team had lost a tough one, but an amazing year for the football team just added another chapter. Later we learned that the Badgers had gathered as a team to watch the show on ESPN. In our radio broadcast, we settled for airing a replay of the announcement, followed by Ron's speech, which I must say was darn good.

There was one other thing that made the night strange. South Florida's home gym was warm, and it was loud. Really loud. Especially right behind us, where for nearly the entire game a woman who obviously was a diehard fan was yelling, "wooooooooooooooooo!" I mean all night long—wooooooooooooooooooo! It was the most distracting noise we have ever dealt with, but what could we do? She paid her money to get in. She was supporting her team. A Tampa newspaper writer seated next to us said she does that game after game. She was a pain in our—ears—but we did give her credit for having vocal cords that allowed her so much hang time.

The Badgers went into conference play with an 8–4 record and then lost four of their first five Big Ten games. For most of the season, they struggled to sustain any momentum. A thrilling victory against 19th-ranked Illinois was followed by a loss to No. 17 Ohio State. They would win a couple more games and then give 'em right back. The up-and-down ways continued when Michigan State came to the Kohl Center and spanked Wisconsin 61–44.

A week later the Badgers lost in the rematch in East Lansing 59–54, but at least the Badgers walked away believing they could play with the Spartans.

From my viewpoint, the turnaround began in Iowa City. For much of the game, it looked ugly. The offense again was badly struggling. Iowa was building a double-digit lead, and Bennett's blood pressure appeared to be rising before our eyes. There was another tough officiating call, and once again, it went against Wisconsin. The Badgers' head coach blew a fuse. On the air I said, "Dick

Bennett has just snapped." He appeared to bump an official, which usually results in an ejection and perhaps a suspension. Neither happened in this case, but there was a strong message waiting for the players.

During a timeout after that incident, assistant coach Brad Soderberg said he told the team that it needed to start caring as much as the coach.

The message must have worked because the Badgers rallied, and the almost always vocal Iowa fans went from cheers to jeers to being plain old stunned. Wisconsin walked off the floor a 54–45 winner, improving their overall record to 14–12. This is not a typo. The record was 14–12. At that time of the season, I was just hoping they could win enough games to earn an NIT bid, but now the Badgers had the spark they needed at just the right time.

A March 1 victory against Northwestern set the stage for the final regular season game against Indiana. This was high-stakes stuff. Now at 15–12, the Badgers were back in the mix for an NCAA bid, but they had work to do. They had to beat Bob Knight's Hoosiers, which history tells us ranges from difficult to impossible. Then they probably needed to do some damage in Chicago at the Big Ten Tournament.

Before the Indiana game, the basketball office was looking for a little athletic department teamwork. That weekend, the Badger hockey team was hosting a series at the Kohl Center. Normally under these circumstances, the basketball team would practice in the Nicholas-Johnson Pavilion, a terrific facility made possible by the generosity of former Badger hoops standout and ultra-successful businessman Ab Nicholas and his wonderful wife, Nancy. It is a valuable part of the Kohl Center, but the day before a game, most coaches want to practice on the arena floor whenever possible. Had this been a game in January, Bennett likely would have had his team in the Pavilion, but for this monster game, he wanted any help he could get.

Hockey coach Jeff Sauer obliged, and on a Saturday morning (the basketball game was on a Sunday afternoon), arena workers, known as the conversion crew laid down the floor, and the basketball team had its practice. I remember Coach Sauer asking me, "Does this really help?" All I could think of was that this team needed any edge it could get, and for a team that averaged less than 60 points a game, if practicing on the arena floor meant one more bucket on Sunday, then yes, it can really help.

Sunday's contest was a CBS-TV feature game with Dick Enberg and Al McGuire on the call. Many years earlier at NBC, those two plus Billy Packer made up college basketball's premier broadcasting trio. Enberg's command of the language, with his famous "Oh, my!" call, combined with the irreverent former Marquette coach and the more serious but amazingly knowledgeable Packer, made for quite the team.

McGuire was just a treat to hear. Bennett had him speak at that year's preseason steak fry, and McGuire needed no notes. He could go in any number of directions, but he was always entertaining. One of his favorite lines was, "Everyone should spend one year driving a cab and another year tending bar. You can learn a lot by driving a cab and tending bar."

He had such an incredible feel for the game of basketball that he probably didn't need to spend a ton of time looking at media guides or game tapes. In fact, he said a big part of his preparation was to talk with a team manager and the team's radio broadcaster. He figured those folks are with the team every day and should have a good feel for what is going on.

A couple of hours before the game, I met with McGuire, and as he did in the past, he wanted me to go down the Badgers' roster and give him one line on each player. When we were finished, we just sat and visited for a few minutes. I never knew him very well, but we had been at a few functions together, and I found him to be extremely friendly. That day he shocked me.

"I think this is it for me. I have had enough," he said.

I gave him a puzzled look. "What do you mean?"

He went on to tell me that he was giving up his TV gig.

"You mean after the NCAA Tournament, right?"

"No, this is it. This is my last game."

Little did I know that Coach McGuire was ailing and thought it was best not to continue. That morning I sat there and tried to talk him out of it, urging him to give the tournament one more run. Later, we found out that during dinner the previous night McGuire told his CBS crew his intentions, and it must have been an emotional evening. Today, fans have their Gus Johnson Moments, but Al McGuire had a few himself, such as his Holy Mackerel call at the end of a 1992 NCAA Tournament game between Georgia Tech and USC. Much like John Madden, who won a Super Bowl as the Oakland Raiders coach, McGuire is known more by the younger generation as a broadcaster and not as a championship coach.

It was McGuire's final game, and what a game it was for the Badgers. Again, the Badgers were down by double-digits, this time 46–34, with 10:46 to play. From there, Duany put the team on his shoulders for awhile, hitting some huge shots. Maurice Linton had a big game as well, delivering a huge drive to the hoop in the final minute.

As time was running out and Indiana was trailing by three, Dane Fife launched a three-point shot, but it was off-target and ended up out of bounds. Truth be told, there should have been some time left on the clock, but the officials did not signal it dead before the horn sounded. After the officials met briefly, they declared the game over. The students stormed the floor. After all, it was a huge win against a team they rarely beat. More importantly, Wisconsin's NCAA hopes were starting to look up.

Knight was ticked. He slammed down his clipboard and then rather quickly composed himself to shake hands with Bennett.

Meanwhile, there was a little scrape at the scorer's table between Otto Puls, who has kept the scorebook for nearly 50 years, and Indiana's Sports Information Director. On paper, the tale of the tape looked like a mismatch. I'm guessing that the Indiana SID had a sizeable reach advantage and was approximately 30 years younger. But never underestimate Otto! In his earlier days he was a Big Ten football official who had to spend a number of Saturday afternoons putting up with Woody Hayes and Bo Schembechler—so our guy Otto was not going to be intimidated by some SID! There was a little grabbing and some harsh words, but after a short outburst cooler heads prevailed.

In the euphoria of the moment, even Dick Bennett allowed himself to enjoy the day. In Mike's postgame interview with the coach, Mike asked Dick whether he was confident about the Badger's NCAA chances. Dick responded that he believed the Badgers were tournament worthy. A lot of us were not quite so sure, but I enjoyed hearing Bennett state his case. Just about every other coach does, so why not the Badgers' boss?

The win gave the Badgers an 8–8 Big Ten record (16–12 overall) and a sixth-place finish, which meant they had to play on Thursday against Northwestern, the team that had finished last in the league at 0–16. Before we taped our pregame interview, Dick was noticeably nervous. I asked him whether he still believed Wisconsin was in good shape for a bid. He admitted that it would be a good idea not to lose to the Wildcats. That made sense, as a loss against such a poor Northwestern team would leave a lousy last impression on the tournament selection committee.

There was very little that was pretty about the game, but the Badgers moved on with a 51–41 win. The next night they beat Purdue 78–66, and they appeared to be in excellent shape. In the tournament semi-finals—a preview of coming attractions—Michigan State eliminated Wisconsin 55–46, but Bennett's team had earned a bid as the eighth seed in the West Regional.

In the days leading up to their first-round game against Fresno State, some players faced the predictable questions about Wisconsin's NCAA Tournament failures against Texas in 1997 and the disaster of 1999. If those questions or the pressure of tournament play itself bothered this team, the players kept those concerns very well hidden.

As the Badgers were going through their pregame warm-ups, Jon Bryant started what I guess you could call a little ritual of coming up to our broadcast position and saying hi. Mike and I were already on the air, and we were caught off guard. Just as we were setting the scene for the game, J.B. stopped by to offer a handshake and ask, "How's it going guys?" That was a decent indication that this group was fairly loose.

On that night in Salt Lake City, Jon Bryant started a hot streak for the ages in Wisconsin basketball. For the season, Bryant averaged eight points a game. En route to winning the West Regional's Most Outstanding Player award, he doubled his average. Down seven early in the second half, Wisconsin punched back with a 14–3 run. Suddenly, Bryant started raining threes, hitting four straight from the left wing. By the end of the barrage, Wisconsin led 61–46, an eye-popping 26–4 run. Bryant, who came off the bench, led the way with 21 points, hitting 7-of-11 shots from three-point range, and Wisconsin had its first NCAA Tournament victory since 1994, 66–56.

I say the team appeared calm beforehand, but one has to believe that game took a lot of weight off of the players' shoulders, not to mention Bennett and his staff. Now all they had to do was beat the region's No. 1 seed, Arizona, a team featuring future NBA players Luke Walton, Gilbert Arenas, and Richard Jefferson.

During the Friday news conference, the Wildcats appeared to be a confident bunch, and with good reason. Even without big man Loren Woods, who was out with an injury, this team had plenty of talent. But the guards were young, something the Badgers were able to exploit. While Andy Kowske delivered a double-double of

10 points and 12 rebounds, Mike Kelley was being his usual pesky self. He scored eight points, but also came through with five steals. Overall, the defense forced 17 Arizona turnovers, holding the Wildcats to 39 percent shooting. Meanwhile, the team that often struggled to shoot straight, the Wisconsin Badgers hit 49 percent from the floor and had four players in double figures.

Wisconsin bolted to a 17-point lead in the second half. Arizona tried to mount a late rally but could get no closer than five points the rest of the way. The West Region's top seed went down, and suddenly the Badgers, who fought just to make the tournament, found themselves in the Sweet 16.

As the excitement was building, and as media coverage increased, the players were embracing everything. In keeping with the "Know who you are theme," Kelley gave me one of the better lines I have heard in an interview. "They are introducing the starting lineups, and I tell J.B., 'Hey, how about this? Two slow white guys are playing in the Sweet 16!'"

By now, a popular T-shirt fans were wearing captured the identity of this squad. "Our Defense is Offensive" it said. Was it ever. Just ask fourth-seeded LSU. This was a very good team, but much like Arizona, the Tigers had young guards in, Torris Bright and Lamont Roland, and Wisconsin was able to take advantage. The starting guards combined for nine turnovers. From our courtside seat, we noticed that LSU players were barking at each other in the first half, but the Tigers could not buy a bucket. Late in the half, Bennett inserted Julian Swartz, who had appeared in fewer than half of the team's games all season. Swartz made the most of his two minutes that night, scoring a basket that helped Wisconsin to a 22–14 halftime lead. That might sound like a football score, but I doubt Badger fans were complaining.

In the second half, the Badgers extended the lead to 18, and while they were not exactly filling it up offensively, the game was a nightmare for LSU—23 turnovers compared to 17 buckets, as the Badgers were now one step away from the seemingly unthinkable.

Earlier that night, Purdue had beaten Gonzaga, setting up an all–Big Ten regional final. While the Badgers had knocked off Purdue twice already, this is the same program that between 1978 and 1990 had beat Wisconsin 26 straight times. The last decade was better, but history was still very unkind. Would this season be different?

Purdue was led by Brian Cardinal, who has gone on to have a long NBA career highlighted by winning a championship with the Dallas Mavericks in 2011. The Boilermakers also had a good, solid guard in Jaraan Cornell, but Kelley simply hounded him. There was genuine reason to believe that Wisconsin could win the regional.

During the news conference the day before the game, Bennett was putting on another good show, giving the media the story of how he came up with his "blocker/mover" system of offense. He told the scribes and the broadcasters that Wisconsin is a football state and everyone loves the Packers, so why not use a football term? I was standing in the back of the room and just watched as national media members were hanging on every word and frantically taking notes.

Bennett did have one line that Mike and I remembered and brought up during the broadcast. When asked about his thoughts on making the Final Four, Bennett told reporters, "I get shivers." And there he was, 40 minutes away from realizing a dream.

As he did throughout the tournament, Bryant stopped by to say hello as Mike and I were having our pregame banter. As the game began, J.B. wasted no time heating up. He scored the team's first nine points by splashing three triples. For the game, he hit five from long range en route to a game-high 18 points.

A late bucket at the end of the half cut Wisconsin's lead to three, 31–28, and the Boilers were getting a little mojo. In the second half, the foul count was working against the Badgers, and I was starting to have my doubts. With 12 minutes remaining, Wisconsin picked up its fifth foul, while Purdue had just two. So many times I had seen Purdue break Wisconsin's heart, from a couple of close losses in the Yoder era to that gut-wrenching double-overtime defeat in 1993 under Stu Jackson. All I could think was, *It's happening again.* Purdue briefly led 50–49, but Bryant stuck a three from the right corner, giving the Badgers the lead.

Back and forth it went. With five-and-a-half minutes remaining and a ticket to the Final Four at stake, Wisconsin and Purdue were tied at 52. The Badgers put together a little burst as Kowske scored on a layup and Boone knocked down a pull-up jumper. Vershaw and Boone each followed with a pair of free throws, giving Wisconsin an 8–0 run.

Yet they just could not put the game away. On a breakaway as Roy Boone was taking it to the rim, he seemed to lose the handle and airballed a layup. Free throws became an adventure as they made just 13-of-24—not exactly the recipe to win a close game. Give credit to Gene Keady's team. As usual, they were a bunch of tough nuts, and players such as Cardinal and guard Carson Cunningham refused to fold.

In the closing seconds, Cunningham nailed a three to pull his team within three at 63–60. At the other end, Mike Kelley was fouled, and with Wisconsin in the double bonus, the heart and soul of the team had a chance to make it a two-possession game. On the air, Mike said that Bennett "has waited 35 years for a trip to the Final Four. What's 10 more seconds?" To which I responded, "He's aged ten more years. This will seem like ten more years."

Kelley split the free throws to make it 64–60, and as the final seconds ticked away and Purdue missed a final shot, the impossible became very real. I am not much into pre-planning what to say in such moments, so I just blurted out, "I'm can't believe I'm going to say it, but here it comes—the Wisconsin Badgers are going to the Final Four!" Not exactly an Al Michaels "Do you believe in miracles?" line, but it was the best I could do.

In previous years, Bennett had themes for each season. That season it was "Touch the Dream." "Now they can live the dream of every college basketball player in America," I said. "The Wisconsin Badgers have punched their ticket to Indianapolis."

The scene was unforgettable. A couple of Badger players jumped on a courtside media table and waved to their deliriously happy fans. During a commercial break, the writers and other broadcasters were making their way to the interview room. Among those walking by our table was Michael Bauman, who at the time was with the *Milwaukee Journal Sentinel* (he now writes for MLB.com). As we looked at each other, all I could do was shrug my shoulders, as if to say, "Don't ask me how they did this."

It was an incredibly special day. Assistant coach Brad Soderberg was our postgame guest, and he told the story of that afternoon at Carver Hawkeye Arena, when the Badgers looked to be on the edge of falling apart, and how the season started to turn.

"There was a stretch where we were really reeling," he admitted. I remember he needed a moment to compose himself. A team that appeared on the brink of a disappointing season was now headed to the Final Four. How it had all changed in less than one month.

Soderberg also told us about the West Regional's Most Outstanding Player, Jon Bryant. When the Badgers brought Bryant into the program, Soderberg said Bryant told him, "I'm just a Division II guy." He was a Division II guy, but he could shoot. "Shooting threes doesn't have a division," the assistant coach told Bryant.

That 2000 team might not have been the most physically gifted, but it was tough and it was smart. The players paid attention to detail. They took note of what the opponents had to say.

"Our kids listened to the Purdue kids," Soderberg explained. "They [the Boilermakers] talked about starting fast. Our players said, 'Why don't we start quickly?'"

Which they did, then they held off a Boilermaker's rally.

On the floor, the celebration continued with players going through the time-honored ritual of cutting down the nets. Watching every member of the program, especially the head coach, take part in that ceremony is something no Badger fan should ever forget. A few weeks earlier, I wondered if the Badgers would play in a post-season of any kind. Now there they were, at the Pit in Albuquerque, New Mexico, as the West Regional champions. In addition to Bryant being named the region's MOP, Mike Kelley and Andy Kowske also earned spots on the region's all-tournament team.

After the game, Bennett mentioned that the only negative to the day was that Wisconsin's victory came at the expense of Gene Keady, who was denied a trip to college basketball's biggest stage. I believe he truly meant those words. Bennett always had tremendous respect for his coaching counterpart. He appreciated how Keady had built the Boilermakers program, which in large part was built on toughness. Yes, through the years there were plenty of star players, but I always figured that to at least some extent, Bennett wanted to follow the blueprint that had worked so well for Keady.

A couple of hours after the game, our radio crew met the team, and a lobby full of Wisconsin fans, at the team hotel where we waited for the buses to take us to the airport. It was a mad scramble to find a TV to watch the Michigan State–Iowa State regional final from Auburn Hills, Michigan. The Spartans had rallied to take the lead, and near the end of the game, Cyclones coach Larry Eustachy was thrown out of the game, an ugly ending to a bitterly disappointing day for ISU.

Unfortunately for the Badgers, Michigan State's victory set up a national semi-final matchup between these two Big Ten teams. It is fair to wonder what might have happened had Iowa State held on to beat MSU. For that matter, there are those who believe that in the Final Four, the Badgers drew the one team they simply could not defeat. In my years calling Wisconsin basketball, I would argue that the 2000 Michigan State team was the best I have seen in the Big Ten. Tom Izzo's group could play any way you wanted. You prefer a track meet? The Spartans will outrun you. You want to grind it out? MSU could do that, too, led by guard Mateen Cleaves, who for my money, is as good a leader as any opponent Wisconsin has faced in the last 25 years. In that semi-final game, he went 1-for-7 from the field, but he knocked down 9-of-11 free throws. Along with players such as Morris Peterson, MSU just had players who found a way to win. It was a puzzle the Badgers could never solve.

There was a light moment in the open practice the day before the game. Near the end of those workouts, many teams like to entertain the fans by putting on a little slam dunk show. With the Spartans, Florida, and North Carolina at the RCA Dome, there were players who could give you some great highlight reel material. Then it was the Badgers' turn. The team that made it to Indianapolis largely by its defense may have made the lowest percentage of dunks in Final Four history. It got to the point where Bennett started chuckling, and eventually the boys mercifully gave up. One more time, "Know who you are," came to mind.

● ● ●

On semi-final Saturday, the Badgers hung in for a half, trailing just 19–17. After the game, players such as Mateen Cleaves admitted to being frustrated at not being able to pull away. In the second half, they did. Jon Bryant's hot streak ended courtesy of Charlie Bell and crew, who held J.B. to just one field goal all day.

Roy Boone was the lone Badger in double figures with 18 points, including a circus shot near the end of the game. Early in the second half, State popped out to a 13–2 run, and from there the Spartans never really had to look back.

In a grind-it-out game, the Spartans hammered Wisconsin on the glass 42–20 and outscored the Badgers at the free throw line 19–7. Otherwise, the game featured a ton of missed shots, which was a shame.

One of the things that bugged me about the Final Four is you often have media members in attendance who rarely cover college basketball, and they had very little knowledge of Wisconsin's story.

They just wanted to be entertained, and frankly, that game was not overly entertaining. As a result, there were some who rather harshly popped the Badgers' program and Bennett's style of play.

Call me biased, but while I get it that many people don't like watching a game with scores in the 40s and 50s, I do believe there are those who missed a great story. Since World War II, there have been two seasons in Wisconsin basketball where there was not at least one player who earned a minimum of honorable mention All-Big Ten recognition. The first was 1946. The other time was the 1999–2000 season. Yes, a team that made the Final Four did so without a so-called star player. Maybe they were not all "slow white guys" as Mike Kelley joked about, but this was a group that, perhaps above all others, was the perfect example of how the whole means more than any individual part.

To me, that makes for a great story.

9

Talkin' About My
"Violation" (And Other Lowlights)

I AM UNSURE WHETHER IT WAS COMMON PRACTICE, but for recruiting visits it was not unheard of for a coaching staff anywhere in America to have someone record a mock play-by-play broadcast, featuring a recruit or a group of prospects leading good old State U to a great victory. As NCAA rules started to tighten, few people were certain as to whether such a practice was a violation.

When Stu Jackson was the coach, I put together something for a high school star out of Fall River, Massachusetts, named Chris Herren. I do not remember many specifics from my make-believe game, but it is safe to say that Herren scored a ton of points in helping the Badgers to a big win. Herren's visit, and listening to that recording, impressed him so much that he enrolled at Boston College. He eventually transferred to Fresno State. (Note: Herren's life was marred by drug problems. His brief NBA career had stops in Denver as well as Boston. To his credit, Herren is believed to be clean these days, and he runs a camp called Hoop Dreams, where he stresses not just basketball fundamentals but the importance of taking care of your body.)

Fast forward to the Dick Bennett Era, and again, yours truly recorded another fake broadcast, this time featuring prospects Mike Kelley, Andy Kowske, Mark Vershaw, and Maurice Linton. (Roy

Boone later joined the team after a stint at Coffeyville Community College. He played at Wisconsin for two years, beginning with the Final Four season. Jon Bryant first attended St. Cloud State before arriving in Madison.)

In this mock game, the Badgers won in dramatic fashion, and the victory earned the team a trip to the Final Four. I could not help but think, *Only in a fake broadcast will this school ever get to a Final Four.* It takes a long time to do these mock broadcasts. After all, it is not done courtside but in a production studio, which is not exactly the best place to capture the emotion of a major sports moment. I had some crowd noise on an old reel-to-reel tape that I would turn up for a big play. It must have taken about 20 attempts to get a tape that sounded even somewhat realistic. I just know I was losing my voice, and I probably sounded foolish while doing play-by-play on something that I was largely making up on the fly.

Fast forward again to March 25, 2000, in Albuquerque, New Mexico. After the Badgers had beaten Purdue to punch their ticket to Indianapolis, we were boarding the plane that would take the travel party back to Madison. As I was getting ready to go up the stairs into the aircraft, someone said to me, "Hey, remember that tape? The guys were laughing about it. I guess it came true." So there it is—my small role in helping the Badgers to the Final Four! (Just kidding, believe me.)

I had forgotten about that tape until someone informed me that it was a minor NCAA violation. Apparently another Big Ten coach reported the infraction, and the enforcement folks let Wisconsin know about it. It's not exactly point shaving, academic fraud, or under-the-table payments, but the UW did discover that it was something the NCAA frowned upon. In case you are wondering, no, I have not put together another mock game, nor have I been asked since that phony Regional Final–winning broadcast. My career as a studio play-by-play guy ended with a Wisconsin victory.

Lesson Learned: never assume the NCAA has enough rules.

If you are in this line of work long enough, there will be things you say on an actual broadcast that you really wish you could take back. Maybe you have heard the comparison between live broadcasting and walking a tightrope without a net. There is some truth in that, and I have had my share of embarrassing episodes.

The year before the Badgers run to the Final Four, they had a nightmare NCAA Tournament game in Charlotte, losing to Southwest Missouri State (now called Missouri State), 43–32. It was an awful performance, and the first half was especially difficult to watch. The halftime score was 21–12, with the Badgers having the 12.

I just remember so many missed shots, then all of a sudden the clock struck zero and Wisconsin had managed all of 12 points.

We were in a commercial break, and we figured our microphones were off—or so we thought. During the break, CBS-TV sent someone to our table for the following question, "Do you remember the halftime score of the Rose Bowl?" He was referring to the 1999 Rose Bowl when Wisconsin beat UCLA 38–31. The halftime score of that game was 24–21. It did not take a genius to figure out what CBS had in mind. I could just see the graphic comparing the football score with the basketball score, or lack of it.

At that point, all Mike and I could do was resort to some gallows humor about the first 20 minutes while we *thought* we were in a commercial break. Mike asked me, "Is halftime longer in the NCAA Tournament?" We figured maybe the Badgers would just decide not to come out for the second half.

I started to laugh. Then I chimed in, "Yeah, I think they are just going to apologize to the city of Charlotte." Yuk Yuk Yuk. Then I gave this parting shot, "I'm sure Duke is really impressed watching this crew." The Blue Devils also had a first-round game in Charlotte later in the day. More chuckles from the broadcast crew.

We'll be here all week—just be sure to tip generously.

The commercial break ended, and Mike and I went back to work, explaining how we hoped the Badgers could find their shooting touch in the second half and all that other good stuff. Obviously, they didn't, and everyone went home the next day. We still had no idea that our "open microphone" halftime performance went over the air—until Sunday.

I picked up the *Milwaukee Journal Sentinel,* and columnist Bob Wolfley had a little story about it. At first, I thought, *Did we utter a four-letter word? No way. We are very careful to avoid that.* Really, we are, so that was not the problem. Our poor man's comedy club routine was the issue. We committed the cardinal sin of broadcasting—we assumed the microphones were off. Turns out the studio board operator forgot to kill our headsets while he was playing the commercials. As a result, our voices were heard over the spots. If I was looking for someone to blame, all I needed to do was find the nearest mirror. That was on me.

At first I started to sweat. "What kind of trouble are we in now? Will they really be that sensitive? I mean, it was a terrible game, right? At least there were no F-bombs." I had to agree with Wolfley, who sort of gave us credit for being honest, even though he knew we assumed we were off the air. I thought it would be best to tell our bosses right away, so I made my confession. As it turned out, it was no big deal. A couple of players and assistants were even able to chuckle about it. At the time of our open-mic trick, the Badgers had bigger worries, like how to score a few more points.

Lesson Learned: Always assume the microphones are "hot."

• • •

Another lowlight was an incident that we kept off the air, but we did give some writers seated behind us a good show. Again, it was during the NCAA Tournament. Notice something of a trend here? This time it was 2005 in Oklahoma City. The Badgers were playing Northern Iowa. Often in the tournament, media members will not be at their courtside seats for much of the game. They could be in the media room for a news conference following the previous game, or they could be writing, or they could be eating. We are really good at eating.

Space can get tight by the floor as tournament officials try to fit everyone covering the game into a limited area. A writer was assigned to our immediate right, but he was not in his seat for the entire first half. His chair wasn't even there. As the second half was unfolding, the game was getting close, and suddenly the writer showed up courtside. I was calling the game when I heard a little commotion. Out of the corner of my eye I noticed Mike had removed his headset and was having words with the writer—while the game was in progress. It seems this scribe thought we were trying to squeeze him out.

We went into a commercial break—yes, the microphones were turned off—and I started verbally unloading on this writer. The writer all 5'6", 140 pounds of him soaking wet was not backing down. I then offered to beat the hell out of him "in front of 18,000 people." Back and forth we went until eventually our engineer, Dave McCann, warned me that the break was almost over. After the little bark fest, I went back on the air as if nothing had happened. Right after I threatened the guy, I said something to the effect of, "15:48 remaining, with the Badgers leading," etc.

The little temper tantrum continued through the next break, when I turned around and noticed Wisconsin writers Tom Oates and Jason Wilde had a front row seat for this sideshow to the basketball game. "Who is this guy?" Wilde asked. "I don't know," I answered. "Check the obits tomorrow." Then it was back to the broadcast.

Finally, cooler heads prevailed. I was pretty peeved that some newspaper writer would interrupt us while we were on the air, accusing us of losing his chair. The writer was pretty peeved when he thought a couple of radio slugs were trying to squeeze him out of his courtside seat. I am leaving the writer's name out of it—he actually is a pretty good scribe, and once everyone calmed down, he seemed like a decent enough person. At a tournament a couple of years later, he was assigned next to us again, giving us a good laugh and giving some other Wisconsin media members an excuse to encourage some courtside fisticuffs. Ah, the pressures of the NCAA Tournament.

Lesson Learned: Make sure those who are assigned near you on media row have a chair.

• • •

Another not-so-proud on-air moment happened when I allowed frustration to get the best of me during a long day of football in Iowa City. It was 1996, Ron Dayne's freshman year. The Badgers had lost their first four conference games—three in heartbreaking fashion. The gold medal winner of lousy endings occurred in a 34–30 stunner to Northwestern, when the Wildcats recovered a fumble in the final couple of minutes. The Badgers were trying to run out the clock when a poor exchange between Mike Samuel and Ron Dayne resulted in a crucial turnover. Northwestern eventually scored in the closing seconds, sparking an uproar from fans who thought Wisconsin's offense could have just taken a knee (had the Badgers gone that route, they would have had to punt, but that topic has been debated forever and a day).

After starting Big Ten play 0–4, Wisconsin was showing signs that it would recover by beating Purdue and Minnesota. Going into Iowa, there still was a chance at a .500 conference finish, which would have been quite an accomplishment after such a rough beginning. The game at Iowa could not have gone worse. The Badgers were a run first, run second, and often, a run third team. Only that day they could not run at all. The Hawkeyes had Dayne throttled, and they hammered Wisconsin 31–0. Needless to say, there were very few highlights for Barry's TV show the next day.

As the game was winding down, the people in our booth noticed a group of Iowa fans in a suite next door. It became clear those folks were having some fun at our expense. Knowing we were the

Wisconsin broadcast crew, they just kept looking at us and laughed the day away. They could not have heard us—we did not have much to say anyway. I mean, the Badgers were getting mauled. But these Iowa fans just kept looking at us with big smiles on their faces.

Finally, I had enough. Mike mentioned that the people next door seemed to be in a great mood, with lots of smiles on their faces. "Yeah," I said, "they have a lot of smiles. They just don't have a lot of teeth."

Stay classy, Matt. Stay classy.

Everyone in our booth busted out laughing, probably more in surprise at my comments than anything else. In my 24-plus years of living in Madison, Wisconsin, I have learned all about political correctness. If anything, I usually err on the side of being too sensitive. And there I was critiquing, inaccurately I might add, the dental deficiencies of a bunch of happy Hawkeyes fans.

When we returned home, a fair amount of people said they heard my comments. Some were happy that I would verbally smack down some rival fans, while some other friends suggested that maybe I should grow up. Regardless of what they thought about my cheap shot, I was a little impressed, if not a bit shocked, that there still were some listeners during the fourth quarter of a one-sided game.

Lesson Learned: Try to act like a reasonably mature adult, even when the team you want to win is getting crushed.

• • •

My biggest screw up happened, thankfully, as a college student. While at Ohio State, a group of us in the journalism school called hockey games for the campus radio station. Today, such stations have a good reach, both over the air and on the Internet. Back in the early 1980s, the blowtorch known as WOSR Radio was only available in a handful of dorms. That was a good thing.

I will say that I was an adequate hockey announcer, at least for a college-aged person, but a simple slip of the tongue has me paranoid about ever again trying to call a hockey game. I don't even remember who Ohio State was playing, not that it matters. I was describing an OSU rush when instead of saying so-and-so "shot the puck," I let fly with a word that rhymes with puck—the F-word. So I told our massive audience that so-and-so "shot the f—k." For the next five minutes I was laughing on the air. So was everyone else in the press area within earshot. I could not stop. I did not use the word in anger. I was not drinking before the game. I just slipped, and our little broadcast crew had material for an end-of-season highlight tape.

I enjoy hockey. I can't say I have a lot of knowledge about the game, but I enjoy watching it, and there are times when I think it would be fun to work a game. But I can't get that night as a college announcer out of my head. Wisconsin hockey has a lot of listeners. It also has an excellent Voice of the Badgers in Brian Posick. Those are good reasons for me to leave hockey broadcasts to the professionals. I will let Posick walk that radio minefield of trying to avoid saying the word that rhymes with puck.

Lesson Learned: See two paragraphs above, and mind the puck.

10

Another Perfect Fit

AFTER THE FINAL FOUR, Dick Bennett and I taped one final coaches TV show, where he announced that he would return for a sixth season. I was mildly surprised because there had been some people who thought that maybe five years would be enough. He prided himself, and rightly so, as being a program builder, and he certainly had done that at Wisconsin.

That summer, the team traveled to Italy for a series of exhibition games. International trips can be valuable for teams because they give them extra practice time, not to mention a chance to see the world. However, I believe the trip may have taken a toll on Bennett. At the team's preseason steak fry in October, he casually mentioned to me that he really could not say he was looking forward to the season.

At the time, I just thought he was a little tired and once that the practices started going and the games began, he would be fine. However, three games into the season, and after a thrilling overtime victory against Maryland in the Big Ten/ACC Challenge in Milwaukee, Bennett announced he was stepping down and that Brad Soderberg would take over for the remainder of the season.

There are those who believe Bennett simply wanted to set up Brad for the full-time gig. I really do not know, and honestly, I do not care. I just know the Dick Bennett I saw early that season appeared to be fatigued. It was as though he had conditioned himself for a five-year run, but with the team making the Final Four, he tried to talk himself into going one more season for the senior years of Kelley, Kowske, Vershaw, Linton, and Boone. Early in the season, Bennett simply did not have it in him to go any further.

All of this put Soderberg in a difficult spot, but his team started extremely well, winning eight straight games, including a nail-biting three-point victory against Indiana in the Big Ten opener. Then the Badgers lost three straight, and it was up and down throughout the conference season. Ironically, they finished 9–7 in the Big Ten, one game better than the Final Four squad, but similar to the 1999 team, the tank appeared to be running low at the worst possible time.

The Michigan State curse continued. In mid-January, the Badgers had them on the ropes in East Lansing, but a key missed free throw by Kelley followed by a cold-blooded three-point shot from Charlie Bell sent the game into overtime. It was the only three that Bell hit all day in six attempts. From there MSU rolled to a 10-point win. In the rematch on Senior Night, Kirk Penney somehow banked two shots from the corner to help keep Wisconsin in the game. The first time he did it, Mike Lucas and I just looked at each other and asked, "Did he really do that?" Since our audience is relying on us to paint the picture, it was not exactly textbook radio, but we were as amazed as anyone in the arena. The shot pulled the Badgers to within five, 45–40, with about 7:30 to play. Three minutes later, Penney did it again, cutting the Spartans lead to 47–45.

But the Spartans were too much, and they won 51–47, giving the UW senior class a 1–10 record against Michigan State. In the final conference game, the Badgers did manage to win at Iowa, but in the Big Ten Tournament Soderberg's team was one-and-done, dropping a grinder to Indiana 64–52. It was not a pretty game—the Badgers shot just 38 percent from the floor, and the Hoosiers outscored Wisconsin from the free throw line 26–7.

With an 18–10 record, the Badgers had done enough to earn a third-straight trip to the NCAA Tournament, this time as a sixth-seed, two slots higher than the previous year. They were sent to Boise, Idaho, to play Georgia State, a little-known program led by well-known Coach Lefty Driesell.

At NCAA Tournament sites, each team gets an open practice. After the open session in Boise, the Badgers had a more thorough workout at the old high school of Badgers guard Ricky Bower.

Through the years, I cannot tell you how many practices I have witnessed. Hundreds, and or perhaps a few thousand, which among other things tells you that I might need to get a life. While I consider that an important part of the job, I have never been smart enough to consistently figure out whether a good practice translates to a good game.

I will say in the practice before the Georgia State game, it seemed as though the Badgers were as crisp as they had been in a long time. Even though some people had their doubts about the team's chances in the tournament, there was strong reason to believe the Badgers could do some damage. Maybe not Final Four damage, but they could be difficult to eliminate.

For most of the first half, Wisconsin played like it practiced, breaking out to a 30–14 lead before the Panthers scored the final five points of the half to make it 30–19. Still, the Badgers appeared to be in good shape, leading by 13 early in the second half. Then the game, and the course of the program, started to change.

The old left-hander threw a triangle-and-two defense at Wisconsin, focusing on Penney and Roy Boone. Driesell was taking his chances that he could leave the less efficient shooters open. The plan worked to near perfection. With about seven minutes remaining, Georgia State tied the game at 42, but the Badgers had an answer and late in the game led 49–44. I started to believe they would hang on.

Then disaster struck. Georgia State's Darryl Cooper stuck a three-pointer and was fouled by Boone in the process. Cooper's free throw made it a one-point game with 48 seconds to play.

On the Badgers' next possession, the shot clock was winding down. Travon Davis was driving the lane as though he was looking for a kick out, but Georgia State forced a turnover that led to a bucket at the other end, putting the Badgers behind 50–49. There were 12 seconds to go.

Soderberg mildly protested that Davis was fouled, but he knew the bigger job at hand was setting up a play that could still win the game. It looked like he was able to do just that as Mark Vershaw took an inside feed and was chopped in the act of shooting. There were 3.2 seconds to play. It was the type of moment that makes the NCAA Tournament so popular—high drama of a one-point game with an upstart program led by a veteran coach trying to eliminate a team that had stunned the basketball world the previous March by advancing to the Final Four.

Vershaw was having a solid game with 19 points and five rebounds. As he stepped to the foul line for what I described as "the two biggest free throws of his career," he was a very respectable 7-for-9 at the stripe (86-for-119 on the season, 117 before those throws). In that situation, Vershaw and Roy Boone were players you would have wanted at the free throw line. Those two guys shot more free throws than anyone on the team and made them at a good clip.

Mark's first attempt, which would have tied the game, was short, and the look on his face suggested, "You have got to be kidding me." As almost always happens at tournament games, most of the people in the arena are simply basketball fans and have limited knowledge about most of the teams at that particular location. As a result, they often sit back, enjoy the game, and if it is close in the closing minutes, they pull hard for the underdog. Last year Wisconsin was an underdog. On this day Wisconsin was the favorite, and now it was a team that was hoping to force overtime.

Vershaw's second free throw was long. Georgia State rebounded, and Wisconsin fouled right away, sending GSU back to the line.

Wisconsin secured a missed free throw, but a desperation heave from Penny was no good as the final horn sounded.

Suddenly, the season was over, and soon after, so was Brad Soderberg's time as Wisconsin's head coach. After the game, I had to do something I truly despise, and that is go into the locker room to interview players after an elimination game. During the regular season, many teams, including Wisconsin, keep the locker room closed to the media. Instead, players appear in the interview room for a news conference In the NCAA Tournament, the head coach and selected players will address the media from a podium, but the locker room is open, as well. It was a bitterly disappointed group. Eyes were red, those of the players as well as some family members of the coaching staff.

Vershaw, while heartbroken, faced the media. "That's the situation you want to be in," he said. "I just didn't come through." Of course, the game was decided by far more than Vershaw's missed free throws. Georgia State's triangle-and-two worked its magic, holding Wisconsin in the second half to just 5–18 shooting from the floor and 0–4 from three-point range.

Almost everyone knew that Soderberg likely would not keep his job, and I do not believe anyone covering the program felt very good about it. Athletics Director Pat Richter liked Soderberg, but sometimes in these matters personal feelings need to be moved aside.

Richter decided to make a change, and Wisconsin basketball had another coaching vacancy. The hot name making the rounds was Utah's Rick Majerus, who just a few years earlier led the Utes to the NCAA title game against Kentucky. Even with his Marquette background, Majerus appeared to be a popular pick among much of the Badger fan base.

During those years, in addition to working together on the game broadcasts, Mike Lucas and I hosted a Monday night call-in show on WIBA radio. We asked our audience who they might like to see get the job. In our very unscientific survey, Majerus was getting support, as was Bo Ryan, who, after an incredible 15-year

run at Platteville that included four Division III national championships, had just finished his second season at UW–Milwaukee.

Both Mike and I had some doubts whether the timing was
right. Once again showing my brilliance in such matters, I said,
"I don't know if Pat has seen enough at Milwaukee to make that
move." The fact is Bo walked into a tough situation at UWM, and he
did his usual excellent work with the Panthers. Back in December,
Milwaukee gave the Badgers a run for their money, taking the game
down to the last couple of minutes before falling 55–47.

After our radio show that night, I met up with some folks at a
local restaurant. I will leave their names out, but trust me when I say
they were very well versed on what was going on with the program.
I asked what they knew about dealing with Majerus and what might
be ahead for Soderberg when one of the people in our group finally
told me, "You know who is going to be the next coach? Bo Ryan." So
about an hour after I suggested that this was not going to be Bo's
time, I now had every reason to believe that I was wrong—again.

There were those who thought Richter was out to hire a big-
name coach, but Pat insists he never uttered those words. He has
kidded me and others for speaking for him. He was right. Many of
us figured he would bring in a so-called nationally recognized coach.

Instead, Richter set his sights on the best possible fit for
Wisconsin.

A few days later, the University of Wisconsin introduced Bo Ryan
as the next head coach. For those who have long supported him,
from his days as a UW assistant, to his amazing run at Platteville,
to his last two seasons in Milwaukee, it was an exciting day. I knew
about his record, but I really did not know him well personally. We
had attended a couple of banquets, and I had spoken to him a few
other times through mutual friends, but on a day-to-day basis, I had
no idea what to expect.

In retrospect, it was a real eye-opener that some other Division
I program did not hire Ryan sooner. At Wisconsin, he certainly was

a viable candidate on a couple of occasions, but perhaps the timing was just not right. When Joel Maturi was the athletics director at Denver, he wanted to hire Bo, but the university administration had other ideas. Ryan just seemed to be typecast as a smaller school coach, where his swing offense could flourish. Critics, who obviously have been proven dead wrong, doubted whether Ryan could get major college players to buy into his system.

Maybe that was the perfect setup for what was to come. Adding to the doubt was the fact that the 2001–02 team was hit hard by graduation. Gone were Kelley, Kowske, Vershaw, Linton, and Boone. In addition, Ricky Bower opted to transfer. There were some promising young players, such as redshirt freshman Mike Wilkinson and a true freshman named Devin Harris, but much of the guts of the Final Four team were gone.

The wily veterans were Charlie Wills and Travon Davis, and in the early stages of the season, the transition was bumpy. Right out of the box, the travel schedule was brutal with an opening game in Las Vegas where the Badgers lost to UNLV 74–69. Then it was on to Hawaii for the Big Island Invitational. After beating the host school, Hawaii-Hilo, Wisconsin lost close games to Weber State and the University of Hawaii. In both games, the Badgers went cold down the stretch. That can happen to any team, but a young group usually will be more vulnerable, and that was what happened during those first few games.

The team returned to Madison for about a day and then boarded a plane for Atlanta to face Georgia Tech in the Big Ten/ACC Challenge. Mike and I flew with them, and as we got on the plane in Madison, this looked like anything but a group of happy campers. The only player I remember with a smile on his face was the always good-natured Kirk Penney. He greeted us with his usual, "Hey mates," but most everyone else was trying to catch some precious sleep.

Similar to the NCAA game against Georgia State, the Badgers played very well for a good portion of the night. A Wills layup gave

Wisconsin a 51–31 lead with 15:59 remaining. But the Badgers could not sustain it. I always thought that Bo hated to admit it, but his team simply had nothing left to give. The travel schedule, which took them from Madison to Las Vegas to Hawaii to Madison to Atlanta was too much, even for young legs. They lost that night 62–61. Again, the team went cold in the closing minutes, and the Yellow Jackets pounced on their tired opponents.

"We're lucky they had two long flights," said Coach Paul Hewitt. "They didn't have the gas to finish."

It was on this night that I discovered one of the key reasons why so many of Bo's players will forever love the guy. Behind the closed doors of a locker room, he might verbally undress a player, but when speaking to the media, he refuses to say anything negative about anyone on his team. Different coaches have different philosophies, and as long as the players know the drill, a number of methods can work. I remember one year after the Badgers beat someone at the Field House, someone asked the losing coach about one of his star players who had a rough game. "Well, I guess he was just horse [bleep]," the coach said. That was the nature of this particular coach. He was almost always blunt, but I believe the record shows his players busted their tails for him.

Bo marches to a different beat, and I have to believe it has meant a great deal to his players to know that publicly, Ryan will do what he can to protect them. That Georgia Tech game gave me an example of what many of Bo's friends had been telling me for years.

As can happen with coaching changes, there is a transition period even for people like me. As I have said, Bo and I really did not know each other well. However, going back to his years as an assistant in the late 1970s and early '80s, Ryan knew Mike Lucas quite well, and Mike and I were hopeful that would help cultivate a good working relationship sooner than later. While it was never at all combative, we got the sense that Bo was being a little guarded, which is perfectly fair. If I were in Bo's shoes, I would be the same way.

By early December, on yet another road trip, we started to break the ice, and much more importantly, that first Bo Ryan–coached Wisconsin team started to come together.

That road trip had the Badgers playing at Ohio University in Athens on a Saturday, then they had to take a bus ride to Cincinnati for a Monday night game against Xavier. The first game of the trip had danger written all over it. It was the unusual occasion of a Big Ten team visiting a Mid-American Conference school. Adding to the storyline was the fact that the Big Ten team was still getting adjusted to a new coaching staff.

Ohio led at the half 36–34, but in the second half, freshman guard Devin Harris started to roll, eventually finishing with 24 points. A key play occurred in the final half minute. While leading by just three points, Travon Davis drove to the hoop to give Wisconsin a five-point advantage. A rookie might have led the way, but it was a senior who helped seal the game. In this case, it was a senior many people had doubted would ever become an effective point guard under Ryan. Davis heard the questions, and so did his head coach.

In previous years, Travon's playing time was rather limited, but he was known as a guard with no fear, which sometimes got him into trouble. By his senior year and with a new head coach, Davis became a very effective player, averaging nearly eight points a game with a 2:1 assist-to-turnover ratio. He also added more than four rebounds a game. Not bad for someone listed at 5'10".

After the game it was on to Cincinnati, where on Saturday night Mike and I got together with Mike's longtime friend, former Badgers football star Tim Krumrie and his wife, Cheryl. After starring at UW, Krumrie went on to become one of the more popular players in Cincinnati Bengals history. I know that might sound funny to some, but at one time, the Bengals were actually pretty good, and Tim was among the reasons why. Unfortunately, there are those who best remember Krumrie for breaking his leg in the Super

Bowl against San Francisco. I hated that moment myself—I was sick for Krumrie, and because at one point in my life I was a Bengals fan, I will forever believe they would have won the game with a healthy #69 on the field. Joe Montana would never have pulled off that late-game drive that ended with a title-clinching touchdown pass to John Taylor. Not that I was bitter or anything.

Anyway, it was good to see the Krumries. At the time, Tim was an assistant coach on a poor Bengals squad. The coaches joined us for a little while. Bo certainly knew plenty about Tim, and the chance to talk about things other than basketball might have been good for everyone. Our group had a few laughs, which Tim might have needed more than the hoops coaches. Don't get me wrong, at that point in the season, my hopes were not very high for a big basketball season, but by December it was evident that the Bengals were going nowhere.

Tim set up Mike and me with some tickets for the big Sunday tilt with the Jacksonville Jaguars. The first thing I remember about walking into Paul Brown Stadium was that as soon as we walked through the turnstiles, vendors were hawking beer. I guess if you have to watch the Bengals, you better have a few cold ones. (Note: The Bengals won 17–14 that day.)

On Monday, the Badgers played Xavier, a team coached by Thad Matta, with Sean Miller serving as one of the assistant coaches. The Musketeers were simply a better team, with players such as David West and Lionel Chalmers leading the charge. Xavier never trailed but never really broke away, either. After leading by 12 in the second half, the Badgers cut it to six on three occasions in the final four-and-a-half minutes. They could get no closer, so the Musketeers won 57–48.

At that point, the Badgers were 3–6, but there was some belief that they were starting to turn a corner.

And boy did they ever.

Keep in mind this team had just eight healthy scholarship players. Promising freshman Latrell Fleming had a career-ending heart condition. Fellow freshman Andreas Helmigk blew out his knee during training camp. Ricky Bower transferred. Julian Swartz also moved on. There were plenty of reasons to think this was going to be the classic rebuilding year for UW basketball. In this case, rebuilding meant "not very good" to most observers, but there were signs that maybe the Badgers would not be so bad after all.

Three days before Christmas, Wisconsin throttled Marquette 86–73 as Kirk Penney hung 33 points on the Golden Eagles. A player named Dwyane Wade, who has gone on to be a fairly good NBA player, was saddled with foul trouble. He played just 25 minutes but scored 23 points.

Next was a tough road game at UW–Milwaukee—Bo's former team. No doubt it was an emotional night for Bo and assistant coaches Greg Gard, Rob Jeter, and director of operations Saul Phillips. It was not especially easy for the Badger players, either. In the final 90 seconds, the Panthers led 79–76. Then Penney drained a three to tie it.

Still, Milwaukee was in position to win the game in the closing seconds. The Panthers were working for a final shot—either win it or go to overtime—when Harris made one of the season's bigger plays. He came up with a steal and then drove the length of the floor for a layup with three seconds remaining. A last-second three-point shot from Milwaukee's Justin Lettenberger was off target, and Wisconsin escaped with an 81–79 victory.

That game ended up being a preview of coming attractions. There were so many surprising games and moments that season, ranging from the Marquette game to the upset of seventh-ranked Illinois to a 94–92 overtime shootout against No. 16 Ohio State. But for me, even more than the title-clinching home victory against Michigan, there are two games that I always will remember—the streak-busting victories at Michigan State and at Indiana.

The game in East Lansing was another one of those games where I had a bad feeling before tip-off. The previous game was a frustrating 51–49 loss at Penn State. Sharif Chambliss knocked down five three-pointers to help the Nittany Lions beat his future squad. Bo was not a happy man. I remember the practice two days before the Michigan State game. Outside of postseason play, media opportunities generally are two days before a game, and after that long, hard workout, I was waiting to interview Wills and Penney. They both were dog tired. Making matters worse was the fact that Wills was dealing with a touch of the stomach flu.

Penney was trying to put on a happy face with his, "I'm fine, mate," smile, but he looked spent. As I was chatting with Kirk, I could see Wills sitting in a chair a couple of feet away, and starting to fall asleep. Sick and tired is not be the best combination for anyone heading into an arena where the Spartans had won the last 53 outings.

Sick or not, it was on to the Breslin Center, and knowing that players can get worn down at various times of the year, I asked Bo in our pregame show about the so-called Dog Days of the season. "I don't believe in such a thing," was Bo's response. Always the tough-minded Philly guy—I mean Chester guy—Bo does not want to hear about, nor does he want to talk about who is tired, who is sick, or who is injured. You either play or you don't. Okay, lesson learned. Do not ask him on the air about being sick, tired, or injured.

And play the Badgers did. Down by one in the final minute, Freddie Owens got in the lane and hoisted up a shot that looked to be from the hip. He banked it in, giving the Badgers a 64–63 lead, but the Spartans had a final chance to keep their home-winning streak alive. With two-tenths of a second to play, MSU was setting up a baseline in-bounds pass. I could see Bo giving a tipping motion, indicating that the Spartans could only tip the ball. A catch-and-shoot would be disallowed. Alan Anderson lobbed the ball to Kelvin Torbert, who was flying into the lane. He caught it, ever so briefly, then he released it, making the shot and sending the home crowd into a frenzy.

Again, I could see Bo making the tipping motion, and right away the veteran officiating crew of Tom Rucker, Randy Drury, and Steve Olson knew they had to talk this one over. We had a TV monitor by us, so as we watched the replay, it seemed clear that Torbert caught it and then shot it. Behind us were Michigan State students who were unaware of the tip rule. They were happy because they saw Torbert make the shot before the clock struck zero, which he did, only the shot was illegal.

Bo was confident the shot would be disallowed. He was clapping his hands before the game was declared over.

Rucker's crew was on top of it. After reviewing the play, they waved off the basket. The Badgers had a huge road win, and Michigan State's home streak was snapped at 53. While we were in a commercial break, some Spartans fans were angry and confused. "How could they not count the basket?" someone behind us asked. I then turned to a couple of them and explained the rule. "Really? Oh, well, never mind then," and off they went. Obviously, the Badgers-Spartans rivalry had not really started yet.

The second streak-busting memory took place at Indiana, where Wisconsin had not won since 1977 when Jimmy Carter was in office and Billy Beer was all the rage. I had seen the Badgers lose on Indiana's senior night a few times, including the evening when Bob Knight honored his players, then recited his famous poem that ended with the Hall of Fame coach inviting his critics to "kiss my ass." Poetry aside, the Badgers had some close games with Indiana, but they always came up a little short—until February 13, 2002. Before the game, Rucker stopped by our table to say hi. We talked briefly about the ending of the Michigan State game, and we had a quick laugh over what might have been some hometown game clock work at the scorer's table. Rucker was in his final season, and he always seemed a friendly sort. You also have to respect officials who make the tough call that goes against the home team. The crew made the right call at Michigan State, but it still took some stones to do it.

The game with Indiana also went right down to the wire. In the closing seconds, the Badgers were clinging to a one-point lead. There was a mad scramble for a loose ball with Wills eventually getting a tie-up with Indiana's Jeff Newton. The crowd was screaming for a foul on Wills. Maybe there should have been, but there was not. After the game, Wills simply said, "You do what it takes." It was a key play, but the Hoosiers still had the ball with 1.9 seconds to play. IU set up a last-second shot from Tom Coverdale, but he missed it. At long last, after 22 games, Wisconsin won in Bloomington.

That year four teams were able to hold up Big Ten championship trophies, but after a 55-year dry spell, no Badger fan was going to complain about sharing a title. The door opened for Wisconsin the night before its regular season finale with Michigan. Ohio State lost to Michigan State, giving the Badgers a chance to move into that four-way tie.

On game night, the Kohl Center was buzzing at the thought of a postgame celebration. Although Michigan beat the Badgers in early February, the Wolverines were struggling and would win just four other conference games. The Badgers were hot at just the right time. Going into the last regular season contest, they had rolled off five straight wins.

There was more than the usual number of media types there, including TV stations from Milwaukee. I remember telling a Milwaukee TV reporter that while Wisconsin was in position to make a little history, a loss might have them on the ropes of even earning an NCAA bid.

That might sound crazy, but going into that final game, the Badgers record was 17–11. What if they lost to Michigan and then got bumped off right away in the Big Ten Tournament? A 17–13 mark might make them a little shaky. But there was no need to worry. Kirk Penney and Devin Harris poured in 21 points each, and Travon Davis scored five points, gathered 10 rebounds, and kicked out seven assists. It was a great senior night for him as well as Charlie Wills. Two seniors who had experienced the joy of making the Final Four, then the heartache of a first-round NCAA loss followed by a coaching change. The early part of their final season was pretty bumpy, but to their credit, they were wise enough to believe in Bo Ryan and his staff. Their reward was the chance to hold up a championship trophy before more than 17,000 fans in Madison.

Well before tip-off, the UW athletic department's marketing folks were very quietly making plans for a postgame trophy presentation. Organizing such a program is important, but it is just as important to keep the plans as low-profile as possible. Just ask Michigan State—I'll have more on Banner Night a little later. A head coach, especially Wisconsin's head coach, does not really want to know anything about postgame love fests. He is just trying to figure out a way to beat Michigan.

Wisely, the UW kept the details rather simple. At the horn, as the crowd was rushing the floor, security cleared space for a stage at center court. Meanwhile, Bo said his main concerns were making sure he made it over to Wolverines coach Tommy Amaker, and that the Michigan players could get to their locker room quickly and safely.

In any ceremony involving Bo, it is best for me or anyone else to just give him the microphone and turn him loose. You could ask him a question, but his answer might have nothing to do with the inquiry. On this night he joked to the crowd that I told him we needed to wrap up the presentation, resulting in some good-natured booing. Thanks, coach.

The best moment came when Bo dedicated the championship to every player who has ever worn a Wisconsin uniform. That was a nice touch. As much as Bo likes to use terms such as "the precious present" and "next," he also loves history, and he understood it was important to recognize players of every era. No doubt it meant a lot to them.

The postseason run was fairly brief. After a first-round victory against St. John's, the eighth-seeded Badgers fell to eventual national champion Maryland. Wisconsin was within eight at the break, but the Terps, behind guard Juan Dixon, pulled away in the second half. Wills and Davis, playing in their final college game, performed well. Wills had 17 points, and Davis added 15.

That first team under Bo Ryan finished 19–13, which is about ten more wins than many people, maybe even me, expected. In October, it was fair to wonder how this team would replace so many valuable seniors. When the team was 3–6 in early December, talk of a Big Ten title likely would have brought laughter. Yet this team, using the same starting lineup from Game 1 to Game 32—Wills, Davis, Penney, Devin Harris, and Dave Mader, found a way to win a league title. Wills, Davis, and Penney made school history. It was the first time three players logged more than 1,000 minutes in a single season. For many games, the Badgers used a seven-man rotation. There was little room for error, and given the lack of available scholarship players, there was absolutely no room for any more injuries. This group may have been one sprained ankle away from being in a mad scramble to play in the postseason.

Credit them, and a perfect fit for a coach, for making that 2001–02 season so much better than anyone could have imagined.

11

Back-to-Back

IF YOU ASKED AN AVERAGE COLLEGE FOOTBALL FAN to name the only Big Ten team to win Rose Bowls in consecutive years, chances are that fan would answer Michigan or Ohio State. Maybe that fan would suggest Penn State. In each case, that fan would be wrong.

The answer is the Wisconsin Badgers. I still believe that surprises people, even here in Wisconsin. When I talk to some old friends from Ohio, they love to recall the glory days of the Big Ten, when the Wolverines and the Buckeyes would battle it out every November, with the winner usually heading to Pasadena. I suppose to OSU and Michigan fans, those are the glory days. But the fact is in many of those seasons, including the famous Bo vs. Woody years, Ohio State and Michigan would beat the daylights out of the rest of the league, stage a knockdown drag-out low-scoring game, then go on to the Rose Bowl and lose.

I thought Big Ten commissioner Jim Delany made an excellent point during the retirement ceremony for Barry Alvarez following the Badgers' final regular season game in 2005. Delany told the crowd that prior to Barry's arrival, trips to Pasadena often had a bad result for the conference. The commissioner noted that changed in the 1990s, largely thanks to Alvarez and the Badgers. It was a comment the fans at Camp Randall, not to mention Barry, had to appreciate. The best part is that Delany is right.

When the Badgers stunned the college football world and won the 1994 Rose Bowl, there were those who considered the season a fluke. "It'll never happen again," was a line I heard time and time again. In 1994, the Badgers needed late-season victories against Cincinnati and Illinois to earn a trip to the Hall of Fame Bowl in Tampa. In 1995, Wisconsin finished with a 4–5–2 record and missed a bowl bid altogether. Suddenly, the critics were feeling pretty smart. Slowly but surely, the Badgers climbed up the standings again, and by the late 1990s, they matched up well with just about any program in America.

Before we get to that 1999 season, it might be a good idea to look at how that team grew because 1997 was a significant transition year for Wisconsin football. The offensive line was almost entirely new with the lone exception of left tackle Chris McIntosh. Joining McIntosh were left guard Bill Ferrario, center Casey Rabach, right guard Dave Costa, and right tackle Aaron Gibson. Four of those five players would start together for three straight seasons. The only change was in 1999 when Gibson moved on and Mark Tauscher decided to return for one final year at Wisconsin. He became the right tackle and went on to an excellent career with the Green Bay Packers.

The defense also went through some major changes. The primary starters along the front four were John Favret, Ross Kolodziej, Chris Janek, and Tom Burke. Kolodziej and Favret were together for three years. Donnel Thompson was a young pup at linebacker in 1997, but he held a starting spot for three years.

Those are just a few examples of the stability the team was beginning to create in 1997. Ron Dayne was a sophomore, and quarterback Mike Samuel was a junior. Overall, it was a very young team that ended up winning eight games before being humbled in the Outback Bowl against Georgia.

That '97 squad put together back-to-back heart-stopping victories, featuring game-winning field goals in the closing seconds from

Matt Davenport. The first of those thrillers occurred on September 27 in the Big Ten opener against Indiana. Late in the fourth quarter, things were looking very bleak for the Badgers. Wisconsin faced a fourth-and-15 when Samuel hooked with up Tony Simmons for a game-saving 22-yard completion to the Hoosiers 29-yard line.

After an incomplete pass and a 4-yard run from Dayne, the Badgers had reached the Indiana 25-yard line with six seconds remaining. Alvarez called on Davenport to save the day. The same Matt Davenport who told reporters, "I'm pretty much money from 45 yards in." He was, nailing a 43-yard field goal to give Wisconsin a 26–24 victory. But there was a price to pay. In the excitement of the moment, long snapper Mike Schneck tackled Davenport, and Schneck ended up dislocating his elbow.

The following week Wisconsin was in yet another down-to-the-wire game at Northwestern. Leading 23–22, it appeared as though the Wildcats were going to break the Badgers' heart for a second straight year, but Wisconsin linebacker David Lysek knocked the ball loose from Wildcats running back Faraji Leary. Lysek pounced on the ball at the Badgers 4-yard line.

Once again the game came down to a Davenport field goal, this time from 48 yards away. Making the challenge more difficult was that the game was at night, and the field was moist from the evening dew. As a result, it was nearly impossible to keep the footballs dry, and wet footballs tend to be heavier footballs. There also was the small matter of a new long snapper, as Mike Solwold was rushed into duty.

Earlier in the game, a low snap resulted in Northwestern blocking a punt, which led to a safety. Later, a high snap turned into a Wildcats touchdown. Davenport might be "Money," but the snap was no sure thing.

However, when it mattered most, Solwold did his job. The snap was anything but textbook, as the ball wobbled to holder Tim Rosga, who put it down for Davenport, and "money" did the rest. After the game, Barry Alvarez cracked that the ball took forever to get to the holder, but Davenport came through one more time and the Badgers had turned a potentially crushing defeat into a rousing victory.

That young 1997 team went into a November 15 game against Michigan with a 5–1 record in the Big Ten and a chance to win a conference title. However, when the top-ranked Wolverines came to town, the Badgers were without Dayne, who had to sit out with a badly sprained ankle. Carl McCullough played very well, but Michigan was just too good en route to a national title, winning 26–16.

The following week, Penn State handled the Badgers 35–10, and then came the bowl loss. It was a disappointing ending, but realistically, given how inexperienced this team was in so many positions, a January bowl bid was impressive.

By 1998, Wisconsin was rolling. It was the team Alvarez considers his best. Most of the Badgers' games were one-sided affairs. A notable exception was the October 10 homecoming marathon against Drew Brees and the Purdue Boilermakers. I swear that game seemed like it took five hours (the box score says the game "only" took 3 hours and 37 minutes). Brees attempted 83 passes, completing 55 of them for 494 yards. Meanwhile, the Badgers were not exactly "Air Alvarez," as Samuel chucked it 10 times all night, completing five passes for a whopping 44 yards. The Boilers also sacked him five times.

In the fourth quarter, cornerback Jamar Fletcher became a show-stopper, picking off Brees (one of four interceptions Brees tossed that evening) and returning it 52 yards for a touchdown to put the Badgers ahead for good.

For the Badgers defense, it was all about bending but not breaking. Purdue amassed 494 yards of offense, while Wisconsin managed 229, proving that statistics can lie.

The only blip in the season happened at Michigan where Wisconsin did very little right in losing to the Wolverines 27–10. On three occasions that day, Dayne and Samuel were on a different page, with one turning right while the other turned left. It also was a tough day for an otherwise stellar defense that allowed seven points or less in seven games that fall.

After rolling past Penn State to clinch a tie for the conference title with Ohio State and Michigan, the Badgers won the tiebreaker and were off to Pasadena for the second time in the Alvarez era. Barry had what he wanted—another underdog team in the Rose Bowl to face a UCLA squad that just missed playing for the national championship. Only a regular season–ending loss at Miami prevented the Bruins from playing in the title game. Of course, broadcaster Craig James gave the Badgers even more fuel when he proclaimed Wisconsin the "worst team to ever play in the Rose Bowl game." Perfect.

As good as UCLA was that season, with quarterback Cade McNown and receivers such as Danny Farmer, the Badgers actually had a good matchup against the favored Bruins. Specifically, Ron Dayne and the Badgers' offensive line had a great matchup. Dayne rushed for 246 yards, one yard short of the Rose Bowl record. As I noted during the broadcast, "They [UCLA] can't tackle him." On the ABC telecast, Bob Griese told viewers that Wisconsin had drawn a team that cannot stop the run.

UCLA certainly could not stop Dayne, who would have had the Rose Bowl record were it not for a fumbled center/quarterback exchange in the fourth quarter. The line was in the process of creating a wide-open running lane for Dayne, but he never got the ball in his hands. When UCLA recovered, Dayne did something he rarely did as a player—he showed emotion. He literally was hopping mad because he knew that had the exchange been clean, he was going to hit the hole for another big run.

As it was, the game, which featured 1,035 yards of offense, came down to a couple of huge defensive plays in the fourth quarter. With Wisconsin clinging to a 31–28 lead, Fletcher again delivered with a pick-six, this time returning a wayward McNown pass 46 yards.

With less than two minutes remaining and the Badgers leading 38–31, UCLA faced a fourth-and-3 from the UW 47-yard line. That is the kind of situation a player lives for. It is also the kind of situation that a broadcaster enjoys.

As McNown dropped back to pass, Wendell Bryant broke through and sealed the game with a sack. "Bryant got him! Down goes McNown!" I blurted. If you watch a replay of the game, you can notice the TV camera shaking a bit, no doubt from the 55,000 Badgers fans who made their way to Pasadena. The Wisconsin Badgers were Rose Bowl champions again.

Naturally, there is going to be some personnel changes from year to year. Wisconsin went into 1999 with a new quarterback, Scott Kavanagh, and a new fullback, Chad Kuhns. On defense, Tom Burke, who was record-setting good in 1998, was gone, as were linebacker Bob Adamov and safety Leonard Taylor. Still, most of the core of the '98 team returned the following season, and hopes were high in Madison.

Ironically, while there were high hopes and expectations in Wisconsin, the Badgers were not favored to win the Big Ten. Alvarez always would crack that in any given year, Michigan, Ohio State, or Penn State would be favored, and he was right. Maybe the quarterback question prevented some pundits from picking the Badgers again, but clearly the '99 club had the makings of being something special.

The team ended up being extra special, maybe in part because it had to overcome a couple of bumps along the way.

Despite a pair of Rose Bowl victories under Alvarez, there still were some people who questioned just how good this program was compared to other college football powers. Among the complaints was the non-conference schedule, which in 1999 had Wisconsin playing Murray State, Ball State, and Cincinnati. The Badgers rolled through the first two games by a combined score of 99–20.

Up next was a road trip to Cincinnati. The announced crowd at Nippert Stadium that day was a little more than 27,000 fans. The previous week the Bearcats had lost to Troy, so the Badgers looked to have another so-called "cupcake" on the schedule. The problem was Wisconsin lost that day, prompting a *Milwaukee Journal Sentinel* Sunday headline that read, "Choked on a Cupcake." Ouch.

It was one of those days when the Badgers did just enough to lose. They controlled the statistics, outgaining the Bearcats 425 yards to 261, but there were costly mistakes. Dayne lost a fumble that UC recovered in the end zone for a touchback. The killer was in the final minute when a potential game-winning touchdown pass from Kavanagh to Lee Evans was called back by a penalty. It all resulted in a stunning loss for the ninth-ranked team in the nation. The outcome trumped what should have been a huge story that day, as Dayne became the Big Ten's career rushing leader, passing two-time Heisman Trophy winner Archie Griffin.

Among those who hated to see that result was ESPN's *College Game Day* crew, which already had committed to doing its popular show in Madison for the next week's game with No. 4 Michigan.

I remember a theme going into the game—how could Dayne pile up big numbers against lesser opponents but falter against other teams in big games?

The week of the game, ESPN's Curry Kirkpatrick interviewed me, among others, about Dayne. He asked about Dayne's fourth-quarter fumble against Cincinnati and how Dayne sometimes just didn't have it on the big stage. I reminded Curry about Dayne's 246 yards against UCLA in the Rose Bowl. "That's a pretty big stage," I said. Yes, the Bruins were not a defensive juggernaut, but it was the Rose Bowl, for crying out loud. And to be fair, Dayne was not healthy for some other "big stage" games, such as the 1997 season opener with Syracuse in the Meadowlands, and he missed that season's game with Michigan with a sprained ankle.

To be honest, I was getting a little ticked off. I thought maybe it was a case of someone already having the story written, and it was just a matter of looking for a few quotes, or in this case, a few sound bites. Truth be told, Kirkpatrick was a highly respected journalist, and I probably was guilty of being more than a little biased, but I had a problem with people who nitpicked a Rose Bowl MVP. Upon further review, that is how it works in big-time sports—the better the player, the closer the scrutiny.

In the first half, I was feeling fairly smart. The Badgers were behind, but Dayne broke loose for a 34-yard touchdown run to make it 14–9 Michigan. However, in the second half, the Wolverines defense blanked Dayne. He had zero rushing yards as the Badgers fell behind. Late in the game, redshirt freshman quarterback Brooks Bollinger replaced Scott Kavanagh and led the offense to a touchdown to pull Wisconsin within five points. After the onside kick failed, the Badgers found themselves with a 2–2 overall record, 0–1 in the Big Ten, and a trip to Ohio State staring them in the face. Critics of the Badgers and Ron Dayne suddenly had more fuel. However, it appeared the Badgers had a found a quarterback.

Still, things did not look good. Making matters worse was Barry Alvarez's knee. It was killing him. On Mondays and Thursdays I would go into his office to tape various radio interviews (a schedule I still follow with Bret Bielema). It was obvious he was in pain. There would be days he would show me his knee, and it was a grotesque, badly swollen, multi-colored mess. The week of the Ohio State game, he was getting worse. Normally, people noticed that Barry usually sported a pretty good year-round tan. That week, he was pale. He thought he might be getting the flu.

When we arrived in Columbus, it was obvious that Barry was not feeling well. I remember sports information director Steve Malchow telling me that the coach was really sick. I tried to talk Barry out of doing his Sunday morning coach's TV show. "You don't need to be there. We can put something together," I said. I figured a free pass out of dragging himself to a TV station for an 8:00 AM taping would be too good to refuse, but he would have none of it. "I'm fine. I'll be there," he said. Must have been that Western Pennsylvania tough guy coming out of him.

The way the Ohio State game started could not have made him feel any better. When Steve Bellisari threw a touchdown pass to Reggie Germany, giving the Buckeyes a 17–0 lead, I told our audience, "The rout may be on." I had the sense that the season was beginning to fall apart.

I was half right. The rout was on, but it was Wisconsin doing the routing. The Badgers scored the next 42 points. After a pair of second-quarter field goals from Matt Davenport, the Badgers ran all over OSU in the second half, especially in the fourth quarter.

It was a thing of beauty. Dayne ran for 161 yards and four touchdowns. Late in the game I declared, "This bad boy is over." It was the first chance I had to call a Wisconsin football victory against the Buckeyes, and I must say I enjoyed it greatly. By this time, Barry had to work from the coaching booth upstairs, and he loves to tell the story of when he came down on the field near the end of the game, Ohio State fans were yelling at him for running up the score.

Wisconsin 42, Ohio State 17.

Naturally, a game like that made Barry feel better for a while, but it was obvious his knee was getting no better. Fans were used to seeing Barry strike a very confident pose, but the Barry I saw was hurting in a big way—to the point where he needed to get to the Mayo Clinic and be away from his team. He met with the media to explain what was going on, but he was struggling to keep his composure.

To the best of my knowledge, it is the only time Barry Alvarez started to choke up in front of the cameras. There was the physical pain plus the frustration of having to leave his team in the middle of the season. Fortunately, the program was rolling along quite well, and for a short period of time, the Badgers were in good shape to handle such a situation. This scenario came to mind when Michigan State had to play without head coach Mark Dantonio, who suffered a mild heart attack in 2010 after his Spartans beat Notre Dame in overtime. If a program is well run with an established head coach, a team has a fighting chance to get through a crisis.

The Badgers were well prepared, with John Palermo taking over for the game with Minnesota. J.P. made it clear that he would remain focused on the defense, while offensive coordinator Brian White and his group would take care of that side of the ball.

As usual, the game at the Metrodome was wildly entertaining. That is just the way it worked at the former home of the Gophers. The Badgers needed a 36-yard field goal from Vitaly Pisetsky to tie the game with 3:00 left in the fourth quarter. The kick set up the first overtime game in Wisconsin football history.

After the Badgers defense shut down the Minnesota offense, capped by a Jamar Fletcher interception, the UW offense marched to the Gophers' 9-yard line. Pisetsky ended the game with a 31-yard field goal, allowing Wisconsin to keep Paul Bunyan's Axe, and giving the Badgers a 2–1 conference record.

Before the game, some folks associated with our broadcast talked about conducting a phone interview with Alvarez from the Mayo Clinic. While that seemed like a decent idea, the man was pretty sick. As it turned out, doctors had planned to replace the knee that week, but discovered an infection and had to postpone the surgery. The infection explained why Alvarez felt the flu-like symptoms. Everyone decided that it would be best to leave Barry and his family alone.

Turns out his hospital room became a bit rowdy. On more than one occasion, Alvarez said nurses had to come into the room and ask everyone to keep the noise down. There was one media person who was able to get through to the coach. To this day, Barry still laughs at how longtime Twin Cities columnist Sid Hartman was able to reach him. That was not supposed to happen at the Mayo Clinic, but as many people have said, when Sid wants to contact someone, he usually finds a way.

After that game, the Badgers really started to roll. As Wisconsin prepared to face Indiana, Barry returned to his team. The Badgers hammered the Hoosiers 59–0. With the game in hand by halftime,

Barry decided to keep Dayne on the sidelines the rest of the afternoon. I remember being disappointed. "It's hard to win a Heisman
this way," I told our audience. After being shut out in the second half
of the Michigan game, Dayne started to get cranked up. In the second half of the Ohio State game, he was nearly unstoppable, but the
next week against Minnesota, the yards were more difficult to come
by. He finished with 80 yards in 25 carries. I, along with others,
thought it might be a good idea for Ron to pile up some numbers
when he had a chance, and with 167 yards in the first half against
Indiana, he certainly could have put up 300-plus that day. Since
Dayne had made *Sports Illustrated*'s list of Top 10 Disappointments
in College Football, many of us figured a big day could at least get
him back on the Heisman radar.

Barry doesn't work that way, so Ron sat the second half. The
story of Dayne's season is very well documented in Justin Doherty's
book, *The Dayne Game*, and there is no need to recap every step of
Dayne's chase. But on that day against Indiana, I was afraid Ron's
Heisman chances, not to mention his attempt to break the NCAA
rushing record, was taking a hit.

That is probably another reason why Alvarez was such a successful coach. He is smart. He knew the game was well in hand. He
knew his team was alive in the conference race. He also knew there
were four games to go, starting with the following week's test against
a Michigan State team that was allowing less than 40 rushing yards
per game.

It was another romp. On the Badgers' first series, Dayne
blew through the Spartans defense for a 51-yard touchdown run.
Meanwhile on defense, Jamar Fletcher was putting a blanket over
Plaxico Burress. The MSU star receiver had a quiet day against the
Badgers' All-America defensive back, who picked off a pair of passes
and helped Wisconsin to a dominating 40–10 victory.

Fletcher never lacked confidence, and in big games the Badgers
could count on him to deliver. As Alvarez loves to say, "If your

mouth writes a check, your fanny better be able to cash it." Fletch could always cash the check.

While the build-up of Dayne's run for the record was gaining steam, so too was the thought that maybe, just maybe, the Badgers could win another title. After disposing of Northwestern, the Badgers traveled to Purdue for a showdown game with Drew Brees and the Boilermakers.

The image of the Big Ten was changing, and Purdue had a lot to do with it. Joe Tiller brought a style of offense that many doubted would work in the "stodgy" old conference. "Basketball on grass" can't hold up when the weather turns cold, right? Well, Tiller's offense created a ton of headaches for defensive coaches, including Wisconsin's, and I figured it would be another very long, very hard game for the Badgers to win.

Wisconsin got some help from, of all teams, Minnesota. Earlier in the day the Gophers had beaten Penn State 24–23, opening the door for the Badgers to move into a first-place tie with the Nittany Lions. All they had to do was win in West Lafayette, which was easier said than done.

The game had a little bit of everything. The Badgers Nick Davis returned a kickoff 91 yards for a score. Drew Brees was throwing it early and often. Purdue was controlling many of the statistics, but once again Wisconsin was finding a way to stay with the Boilers. The Badgers led at the half 14–7, but Purdue tied the game on Brees' touchdown pass to Tim Stratton. In the fourth quarter, Purdue was back on the move, driving to the Badgers 19-yard line. Then Purdue got a little too cute, trying a reverse pass with wide receiver Vinny Sutherland. Badgers safety Bobby Myers made one of the season's most important plays with an end zone interception.

Dayne did not break the rushing record that day at Purdue, but his final assault on the record sure as heck started there, as did the Badgers' pursuit of another championship and Big Ten history. First, Dayne outran the Boilermakers defense for a 41-yard touchdown. Then for the second straight year, Jamar Fletcher picked off a Brees pass and returned it to the house, this time from 34 yards away.

Purdue had scored to make it 28–21, but the onside kick failed. Needing to pick up one first down, the Badgers did just that with Dayne blowing through safety Adrian Beasley in one of those classic runs that is part of any decent highlight video of Ron's college career.

In my years covering Wisconsin football, there have been three weeks that were just off the hook. The 2010 game against No. 1 Ohio State, the 2011 Big Ten opener with Nebraska, and perhaps above all else, the 1999 tilt with Iowa. The Hawkeyes were a team in transition with first-year head coach Kirk Ferentz and a defensive assistant named Bret Bielema. That year they simply were not very good, and Badgers fans could not have been happier. A rival that is down, Ron Dayne 99 yards from the NCAA career rushing record, and a chance for the Badgers to win another Big Ten title—it was the perfect set-up for an amazing day.

I felt like I was on every radio station in the country that week. That is often how it works in this business. A coach will only do so many interviews. A player will only do so many interviews, and in the case of Dayne, who really did not enjoy media sessions, the UW kept his commitments to a bare minimum. What happens? Stations and networks often end up contacting the radio play-by-play announcer.

One of the stranger questions I had came from an ESPN radio host who asked whether I had planned what to say when Ron broke the record. Maybe some broadcasters do that, but I responded that it is hard to write a script when no one knows how, or even if, he will get there. I knew Iowa was bad that year, but football can be a cruel game. What if Dayne gets hurt in the first quarter? He needed just 99 yards, but maybe the Hawkeyes would rally for one game and prevent such a magical moment.

The day itself could not have been better. The weather was perfect. Penn State had lost earlier in the day, meaning a Wisconsin victory would send the Badgers back to Pasadena. It was setting up to be a perfect day to be a Badgers fan.

One of my favorite parts of game day is the drive to Camp Randall Stadium. I love people watching, and it is always fun to witness thousands of fans decked out in their Badgers garb. Add the smell of brats on the grill, and it is always a good scene. I usually arrive at the stadium about three hours prior to kickoff, and most of the time it is fairly easy to weave through any pedestrian traffic. On November, 13, 1999, it was a slow go. Fans were everywhere, and the last half mile or so of my drive took several minutes.

A friend of mine once told me, "Matt, you have a great job, but you miss one heck of a party on a Badger game day." He is probably right, especially for a game of this magnitude.

As the Badgers' announcer, I certainly can be animated, but with a moment like Dayne breaking the record, I really wanted to keep it simple. Perhaps the ESPN interviewer was thinking I would try some type of Jim Nantz caption, such as when a young Tiger Woods won the Masters for the first time, and Nantz declared, "A win for the ages."

I thought that for radio it was better to just explain what happened and not screw it up. I had nightmares of us going off the air, which is what happened to the San Francisco Giants radio network when Barry Bonds hit his 715th home run, passing Babe Ruth. I was afraid maybe I would get the hiccups, or worst of all, Dayne would fall short and the Badgers would lose the game. After all, Dayne set the UW record on a short run against UNLV. He broke Archie Griffin's Big Ten record in the loss at Cincinnati. There was no guarantee that everything would go perfectly.

But everything did go perfectly. The Badgers rolled, and Dayne and the Badgers made history in the second quarter. When he broke the mark, I stuck with my own plan and kept it simple. "There it is! Ron Dayne has become the NCAA's all-time career rushing leader! The man of few words has rushed for more yards than anyone in Division One history!"

As teammates mobbed Dayne and the photographers took their pictures, I just wanted to somehow summarize what Ron Dayne is all about. He made it easy. Someone tossed him the football, which he calmly flipped back to the sideline. "If ever there's a man who symbolizes a program, it's Ron Dayne of the Wisconsin Badgers."

What I meant by that was simple. He is a blue-collar player. Nothing fancy, and he has very little to say. He just does his job and allows the numbers to do the talking.

I did make one on-the-spot editorial decision. As the crowd continued to go wild, and as the Badgers went back in their huddle, a streaker ran the length of the field. In his book, *The Dayne Game*, Doherty interviewed the streaker, a fellow named Tim Condon. I decided not to even mention what was going on. Call me stuffy, but I did not believe a moment such as Dayne's record-breaking run needed any comic relief.

If Dayne's run was the season's best moment, maybe the second best was late in that game. Barry Alvarez was still working from the press box booth, but as the fourth quarter progressed and the Badgers were in complete control, Barry decided it was time to get down on the field. He started to embrace some of his players, then he and Dayne wrapped their arms around each other in as warm a hug as you will ever witness. It was hard to watch that scene and not be moved.

I have friends in this business who have called national championships games, Super Bowls, and World Series, but I am not sure any of them has had the chance to see a game that had more genuine joy. People often ask me about my favorite memory of covering the Badgers. The good news is there are quite a few, which I will go into later in this book, but I must say that 1999 game with Iowa is hard to beat. The Wisconsin team was left for dead after losing to Michigan and falling behind 17–0 at Ohio State the following week—how it all turned around that day at the Horseshoe.

Barry has said that his 1998 team is the best he coached at Wisconsin. It is difficult to argue with the head man, but I find myself wondering if that 1999 team was maybe just a bit better. The way it rallied against the Buckeyes. How it persevered without Alvarez on the sideline at Minnesota. How it blew out a good Michigan State team, and how it outlasted another Drew Brees air show in West Lafayette. Normally the Badgers are at their best when hype is at a minimum. While they were not everyone's preseason pick to win the Big Ten, most thought they would be a strong contender with a big-time Heisman Trophy candidate leading the way. They made it, winning their final seven regular season games. They finished the championship run when they knocked off Stanford in the Rose Bowl.

That Rose Bowl game was different for a couple of reasons. One, the Badgers were favored. No Craig James comments about a lousy team in the Rose Bowl would apply here. Two, the team had such a long layoff between games that it looked a little sluggish at times, especially in the first half. But it was good enough, with Dayne rushing for 200 yards in his final college game, for another Rose Bowl MVP award.

"They are back-to-back Rose Bowl champions. It's over," I said, keeping it short and sweet. At the time I am not sure people fully appreciated what the Badgers had accomplished. Mike Lucas and I still laugh when we talk about how some fans wanted to travel to a different bowl—that they had seen the Rose Bowl a couple of times and wanted to try something else. What? While the stadium itself is aging, the area surrounding the Rose Bowl never gets old. I love how it looks by the fourth quarter, with a little haze coming down from the San Gabriel Mountains on a beautiful January day.

Like any number of fans, I grew up watching the Rose Bowl every New Year's Day, and there I was, calling that game, and

Wisconsin players (from left) Victor Meckstroth (59), Joel Nellis (89), and Jason Pociask celebrate their 24–10 victory over Auburn with the trophy and coach Barry Alvarez (right) after the Capital One Bowl in Orlando, Florida, on Monday, January 2, 2006. It was Alvarez's last game as Wisconsin's coach.
(AP Photo/John Raoux)

Bret Bielema leads the Badgers onto the field on Saturday, August 30, 2008, in Madison, Wisconsin. *(AP Photo/Andy Manis)*

Dick Bennett (right) acknowledges the crowd during halftime of the Wisconsin-Northwestern basketball game at a ceremony to commemorate the 10th anniversary of the Kohl Center on Saturday, January 19, 2008, in Madison, Wisconsin. At left are former athletic director Pat Richter and former hockey coach Jeff Sauer.
(AP Photo/Andy Manis)

Coach Bo Ryan (second from right) receives a game ball from seniors Jordan Taylor (11) and Rob Wilson (second from left) on Ryan's 265th win at Wisconsin, putting him in a tie with Harold "Bud" Foster for most wins at the university, after a game against Illinois on Sunday, March 4, 2012, in Madison, Wisconsin. Wisconsin won 70–56. Behind are Josh Gasser (third from right) and Barry Alvarez (right) Wisconsin's athletic director.
(AP Photo/Andy Manis)

After winning the 1999 Heisman Trophy, Wisconsin's Ron Dayne was drafted by the New York Giants. He is shown here in a game against the Green Bay Packers at Lambeau Field on October 3, 2004, in Green Bay, Wisconsin. The Giants beat the Packers 14–7. *(AP Photo/David Stluka)*

Quarterback Russell Wilson (16) carries the ball during a game against Indiana on October 15, 2011, in Madison, Wisconsin. The Badgers won 59–7. *(AP Photo/ David Stluka)*

Guard Jordan Taylor handles the ball during a game against the Purdue Boilermakers at the Kohl Center on January 9, 2010, in Madison, Wisconsin. The Badgers won 73–66. *(Photo by David Stluka)*

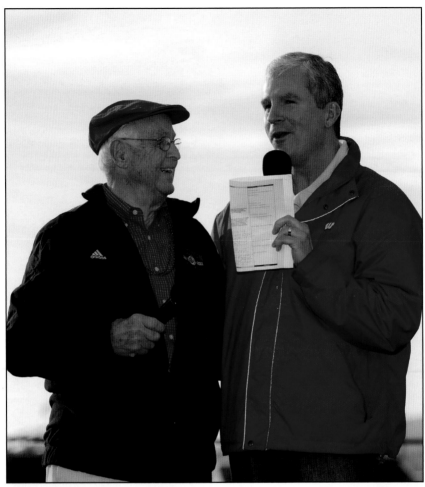

Matt Lepay introduces Wayne Hansen, a member of the 1953 Rose Bowl team, in front of an estimated crowd of 25,000 Wisconsin Badgers fans during the Party at the Pier pep rally at the Santa Monica Pier in Santa Monica, California, on December 30, 2010. *(AP Photo/David Stluka)*

Badgers fans by the thousands were there, as well, cheering on a program that one decade earlier was in disarray. That 1989 team won two games, resulting in a coaching change. The 1999 team won a Rose Bowl for the second straight year, something no other Big Ten team—not Ohio State, not Michigan, or anyone else—has been able to do.

12

Confessions of a Former Buckeye

HAVING LIVED IN WISCONSIN for nearly a quarter century, the friendly nature of people in this state never ceases to amaze me. Even when these folks find out where I am from, or worse, when they find out where I went to school.

Yes, I am a graduate of Ohio State, or as some alums like to say, The Ohio State University. So is my wife. She graduated Cum Laude. For the record, I did not.

Want to know a sure-fire way to get booed at a speaking gig? Have the person who is introducing you tell the crowd you attended Ohio State. At least it is good-natured booing. At least I think it is good-natured booing. A few years ago at a golf outing in Madison, I was in a foursome with Casey Rabach, the starting center on the back-to-back Rose Bowl teams, who has gone on to a very good NFL career with the Baltimore Ravens and the Washington Redskins. Also in our group were two loyal donors to UW Athletics. One of them knew I was from Ohio, and he casually asked if I had attended Ohio State.

"Yes, but I try to keep that kind of quiet around here," I said.

Apparently it was not quiet enough for Rabach, who was standing a few feet behind us. All of a sudden, I heard him clearing his throat. Very loudly.

"You went to Ohio State?" he asked with a disgusted look. He went on to give me his opinion of The Ohio State University, which I am guessing is shared by many on campuses not named The Ohio State University. I should note we finished the round without incident.

One of the more difficult things for some fans to understand is how someone from another school can detach himself from his alma mater. I remind people that Wisconsin's current head football coach played at Iowa, and the Hall of Fame coach and current athletics director played at Nebraska. I doubt when Bret Bielema and Barry Alvarez were in college that they were dreaming of coaching at Wisconsin. Sometimes life just works in mysterious ways.

I can't give you the exact statistics, but it is fair to assume that a majority of major college "voices" attended other institutions. Some are able to stay close to home. In the Big Ten, Northwestern's Dave Eanet and Penn State's Steve Jones are examples of team voices who call games for their alma mater. Otherwise, it probably is a fairly short list, at least with BCS conference schools.

In this line of work, you seek the best opportunity, and for me, that opportunity has been in Madison as the Wisconsin Badgers play-by-play announcer. Having lived here for almost half of my life, I certainly consider myself a Wisconsinite.

Now for the confession, Badger fans. Being from Ohio, there was a time when I really did not like you people. When I was in school, the Buckeyes had a world of trouble with the Dave McClain–coached Badgers. A couple of games stand out. The first was in 1982 at Ohio Stadium. It was pouring rain, but a group of us decided to tough it out and at least go to the game in hopes the rain would stop. Wisconsin scored early to take a 6–0 lead, and the rain was still falling. Being fair-weather fans, our group decided we had seen enough. We figured Ohio State would come back, but we had no intention of sitting through a downpour to watch it, so we punched out.

Our group hit a couple of campus watering holes, then we gathered at a friend's apartment where we turned on the radio and sat there stunned when we heard the game was now late in the fourth quarter and it was still 6–0. Former Wisconsin quarterback Randy Wright likes to tell the story of that game. He was playing with an injured hand that made throwing the ball next to impossible. Wright stayed in the game, but with wet conditions and a bad hand, he spent much of the day handing off. The defense helped him, bottling up OSU all day long.

The score never changed, and we were not a happy group of Ohio State students.

The other game that stands out was in 1985. I was working at WNCI in Columbus, and it was the last Ohio State home game I covered for the station. The Buckeyes had a significant statistical advantage, outgaining the Badgers 365 yards to 222, but Wisconsin forced three fumbles as the Badgers shocked them again 12–7.

I remember the closing minutes of that game, being on the field with other media members. That is what you do when you are not calling the game. In order to get to the postgame news conferences on time, media will leave the press box with five minutes or so remaining, then if the game is close, we will watch the closing minutes from the field. I was standing just beyond the south end zone, near the tunnel Ohio State uses to access the locker room. After the game, as the dejected Buckeye players were making their way off the field, irate fans were letting them have it.

"Chokers."

"You suck."

Those were the polite remarks from a sometimes-very-hard-to-please fan base. In the early 1980s, the Badgers had their way with Ohio State and won four times in five years—a fact UW folks loved to share with me when I first moved to town.

I wish I had a dollar for every time a fan asked, "Is it hard for you when the Badgers play Ohio State? Don't you still have strong feelings for your old school?" In terms of who I am pulling for, no, it is not difficult. Maybe there are some in this business who believe differently, but for me, the appeal of sports is more about the people than the teams.

Let me explain. Growing up, I was a diehard fan of the Cincinnati Reds, the Cincinnati Bengals, Ohio State football, and University of Dayton basketball. Like many, I was a sports junkie, and in my case, I probably was a bit spoiled because all of those teams were pretty good (yes, even the Bengals). Once I got into the business of covering sports, my outlook started to change. Maybe part of that is because I left my home state to pursue my broadcasting ambitions. I have become more of a general sports fan who simply enjoys the games. Yes, I like to see the Packers, the Brewers, and the Bucks do well, but I cannot say that I am a diehard fan of specific teams the way I was in my younger years.

So to address the question of whether it is difficult for me not to have a little bit of rooting interest in Ohio State when it plays Wisconsin, the answer is no. I don't know Urban Meyer or Thad Matta. I have met them both, and they seem like good guys. Obviously both are exceptional coaches, but that is about as far as I can go. Other than broadcaster and good friend Paul Keels and some folks in Athletic Communications, I really know very few people associated with OSU. However, I do know the Wisconsin coaches rather well, and through the years I have been lucky enough to develop very good relationships with a number of players as well as UW administrators both in and out of athletics.

If anything, a Wisconsin–Ohio State game means more to me for purely selfish reasons. I still have a lot of family in Ohio. My niece, as well as a brother and a sister-in-law are OSU graduates. When I go home, is it a little more enjoyable for me when the Badgers beat the Buckeyes? You better believe it is. Let me put it to you another way. When Braxton Miller threw that touchdown pass with 20 seconds left last October, I felt sick to my stomach. I could not believe that Wisconsin would lose consecutive games in such a fashion.

Look, my job is to be Wisconsin's radio announcer, not its head cheerleader, but it does not take a genius to figure out the job of a play-by-play announcer is considerably easier when the team he is associated with is winning. A couple of years ago I spoke to a sports business class on the UW campus, and one of the things I stressed was this—if you choose to do this for a living, you might end up working for someone other than your favorite school or franchise. You might even end up working for a rival. That is just a fact of life.

This is where rooting for people rather than teams comes into play. I never was a New York Jets fan, but when they would win a game, I was happy because Jim Leonhard has been an important player on their team. The same is true for the Cleveland Browns because Joe Thomas is there. A couple of years ago it became a little more tricky because of all the former Badgers assistant coaches who were on the Minnesota Vikings staff, led by then-head coach Brad Childress. Fans in Minnesota and Wisconsin are well-versed on the bitter rivalry between the Packers and the Vikings, and while I preferred to see Green Bay do well, it was hard for me not to have at least some feelings for Childress, Darrell Bevell, Jim Hueber, and all the others who gave so much to the UW program.

At the same time, on several occasions I have bumped into Packers GM Ted Thompson, either on the UW campus or at an annual event at Lambeau Field during the summer. While he tends to win very few points on how he deals with the media, I have found him to be very cordial. He is focused beyond belief, as well. Former Packers President and CEO Bob Harlan has as much class as anyone in sports, and he is a big reason why it is easy for me to enjoy Green Bay's success.

I hope this makes some sense, but don't feel too badly if it does not. It has taken my wife many years to come to grips with the fact that I do not live and die by the Buckeyes. For many years, the week of a Wisconsin–Ohio State game would be a little tense in the Lepay household. There would be times when we decided it would be best if we just avoided each other for a few days. That probably was a good decision, because, you know, those Buckeye fans can be a little mouthy (wink, wink).

"Honey, I represent the University of Wisconsin. Can't you understand that?" I would plead.

"Yeah, right. Go Bucks!" she would say.

Great.

The good news is she finally is starting to change her tune. Maybe it was the NCAA violations that led to Jim Tressel's removal as Ohio State's coach. Also, I believe Linda is one of many who fell in love with the 2011 Badgers football team and that certain quarterback named Wilson. While I would not call her a diehard sports fan to begin with, she really enjoyed going to the home games this past season, and when she can, my wife never minds going to nice bowl games. From time to time, she even wears Badgers gear. I am getting there, folks— and she does love living in Madison, so there is always hope.

At least during the week of a Wisconsin–Ohio State game, we can talk to each other. Sometimes I bring in some reinforcements. My best friend from high school is Scott Rader. He is a Michigan grad. Guess what team he really enjoys seeing lose? For the last few years, Scott and his lovely wife, Terri, have visited us for a home football weekend. I look forward to seeing them again this November when the Badgers host—who else?—Ohio State. By the way, Scott has never seen the Badgers lose in person.

I do have feelings for my old school. As a student, I made many wonderful friends and met the woman who became my wife, but that does not mean I am obligated to root for the Buckeyes on Saturday afternoons in the fall.

Okay, I guess I do have one confession regarding my alma mater. I still enjoy seeing the OSU band perform Script Ohio. That isn't so bad, is it?

13

A Different Perspective

ON MARCH 14, 1992, Wisconsin's basketball team closed out the season with a 76–65 loss at Northwestern. The Big Ten Tournament was still a few years away, so that game might have been the least important of the day in major college basketball. The ninth-place team lost to the tenth-place team, but it is a day I always will remember. Not the game itself. Actually, I have next to no recollection of the game. It is the postgame that sticks with me.

The University of Wisconsin had already announced that Coach Steve Yoder would not return the following season, ending his run as the Badgers' boss at ten years. They had the glorious night against Michigan, when the Badgers drilled the 17th-ranked Wolverines 96–78, but it was all downhill after that evening. The loss in Evanston meant Wisconsin closed the season with five straight defeats, the only close game being a five-point setback at home against Iowa.

In those years we conducted postgame interviews with an assistant coach. Yoder's staff that year was made up of Ray McCallum, Chuck Schramm, and John Williams. It was no secret that all three were about to enter coaching limbo, which would officially start when the horn sounded at Welsh-Ryan Arena. That 1991–92 team finished 13–18 and 4–14 in the Big Ten, so there was no suspense about making a postseason tournament.

By then, Stu Jackson's name was swirling around town as a strong candidate to replace Yoder. That was a much bigger story than a game that had no bearing on the conference standings and no tournament ramifications whatsoever.

Northwestern won, giving coach Bill Foster's team two Big Ten victories on the season. I do remember the smile on his face after the game. Like Yoder, Foster had very little to be happy about that winter, so he deserved to feel good, at least for a day.

While the Wildcats were celebrating a rare victory, Ron Blomberg and I were getting ready to interview an assistant. On that day, it was Williams' turn. In a situation such as this, there really is very little to ask. We talked about the game itself and the seniors playing their final college game—Billy Douglass, Brian Good, Jay Peters, and Jay Schell.

Under the circumstances, the interview was going along well enough. Ron and I wanted to wish Williams and the other assistants the best of luck in whatever direction they were headed. To be honest, most of us around the program believed that McCallum would likely be offered a spot on the next coaching staff, and we also figured Williams and Schramm would move on to other opportunities. At that point in our conversation, it would have been perfectly suitable for John to say thank you and wrap up the interview. Instead, he took a few moments to thank the fans, as well as Ron and me for our friendship during John's three years on the Wisconsin staff.

As he was thanking us, I could see his eyes were getting watery. The last thing anyone wanted to do was start crying on the air, so at that moment I thought it would be best to look away. I turned toward the floor, and I saw Williams' preschool-aged son, dressed in a very nice toddler suit and tie, just walking around by the court, obviously too young to be aware of what was going on with his father's job.

All of a sudden, I felt a genuine sense of sadness and concern. I was lucky to work with Ron Blomberg. He had been around basketball at every level, and he probably has seen just about everything there is to see in the sport. When the UW decided to let Yoder go, Ron gave me a good piece of advice—generally speaking, head coaches should come out of these situations in decent shape financially. If you are going to worry about someone, worry about the assistant coaches.

As we were talking with John Williams, those thoughts were in my mind. Here was Williams, in no way at all looking for a pity party. He was just being a good human being by saying thank you and goodbye to some people he probably would not be working with again. Now he was starting to break down. The sight of his son and the sudden uncertainty of the family's future were getting to me. I thought I would get through the interview, but then I saw Ron, and *he* was starting to tear up.

By then, I had no chance. I started to thank John one more time, but then I just lost it. So did the other two. None of us could say anything, which is never a good thing during a radio broadcast.

There are two very helpless feelings one can get while on the air. One is uncontrollable laughter. You can find that stuff on YouTube fairly easily. The other is when you start to cry. I can say that day in 1992 is the only time it happened to me, but man, that was tough. I never was able to retrieve the tape from that interview, but it seemed as though none of us could talk for the longest time. The reality is the dead air probably only lasted a few seconds.

Whatever the case, I did not care then, nor do I care now. I would not suggest that crying on the air is something every broadcaster needs to do, but that day drove home a lesson that I hope I take with me for as long as I am in this business. As sports fans, it can be very easy to call for someone to get fired. There have been those talk show hosts who make a living being so-called "coach killers." Whatever. To each his own. For me, that March afternoon at Northwestern reminded me that these coaches are just people. Yes, they can make *really* good money, although in the early 1990s, college basketball assistant coaches were not exactly getting rich. That day, it suddenly hit me that a very young boy had a mother and a father whose future was in doubt. I could not help but be touched by that scene.

I am not trying to sound like Pollyanna. There is the old saying that coaches are hired to be fired. Yes, they sign up for this possibility, but when you are around these men and women on an almost daily basis, you have a chance to gain a little different perspective.

I had already seen Don Morton and his staff get fired, but I had only been around them for a year and a half. The basketball coaching change had a different feeling. I had known them longer, plus the staff and the rosters are much smaller, allowing for the chance to develop professional relationships—and in some cases, good personal friendships.

After the 2000–01 season, it happened again. A big difference was Brad Soderberg's final game as Wisconsin's head coach was a stunning loss in the NCAA Tournament, not a battle of ninth and tenth-place teams in the Big Ten. That was no fun to witness.

When Georgia State staged its second-half rally to beat Wisconsin in Boise, Idaho, there was no crying during the postgame show, but Mike Lucas and I both figured we would be working with a new coaching staff the following season. And make no mistake, there were some very real tears coming from the basketball players, staff, and families.

The day after the game, a photo in many newspapers showed Brad's wife, Linda, hands covering her mouth with tears in her eyes, as she witnessed the Badgers' season, and her husband's time as Wisconsin's head coach, slipping away.

In taking over for Dick Bennett three games into the season, Brad was in a brutally difficult position. I had the feeling he knew it would take a good postseason run to keep his job, but there also was reason to believe it could happen. Not knowing what direction the

UW would take with its next coach, most of us close to the program were hoping for another big tournament run.

That collection of coaches plus the senior class made for a very close group. I enjoyed spending time on the road with the staff, especially assistants Shawn Hood, Brian Hecker, and director of operations Paul Costanzo. Mike Kelley's father, Tim, often would join us, and we always had a few laughs on a cold winter night in some Big Ten town.

On the afternoon of March 15, 2001, reality set in that those days were about to end. Pat Richter could not help but feel some compassion, suggesting to reporters after the game that your heart might tell you one thing, but your head might say something else. Everybody liked Soderberg and his staff. Everybody liked the players, especially that senior class of Kelley, Vershaw, Kowske, Linton, and Boone.

On two occasions, coaching changes led to difficult postseason banquets. The 1995 banquet was going to honor seniors Michael Finley, Brian Kelly, Andy Kilbride, and Chris Conger. Richter was in a delicate position—should he attend the banquet right after dismissing Van Gundy? Or would it be better to stay away and let the team have its banquet without him?

In what was probably a lose-lose scenario, Pat and other administrators opted to stay away. I think Pat was just trying not to be a distraction, but the decision did not go over very well with some members of the program. The outgoing coach was unhappy. Some of the players were unhappy. Their final season was a disappointment, and the banquet was a less-than-grand conclusion for a class that helped the program to its first NCAA bid in 47 years.

There was a bit more activity during the banquet following Brad Soderberg's dismissal. After the Georgia State game, a reporter asked Mike Kelley for his thoughts on Soderberg's future. To the surprise of nobody close to the program, Kelley strongly supported his coach. I took it as a player, a team leader, standing up for Soderberg—nothing more, nothing less.

Obviously, Pat made the coaching change and this time he attended the banquet. Probably not his first choice on how to spend an evening, but he was there. Not at the head table, but he was in the crowd.

Before the banquet, Dick Bennett told me he had a few things to say. He wanted a simple, non-descript introduction. The evening was going along well enough. As you might imagine, there was some sadness, but there also was, under the circumstances, at least the appearance of an upbeat environment. It was good to see the players and coaches attempt to celebrate the accomplishments of a senior class that made so much magic a year earlier.

Then the time came for me to introduce Dick. I simply nodded to him that it was his turn, and to the surprise of almost everyone in the room, Dick walked up to the podium.

From there, he went into a passionate talk about the state of the program when he arrived and how much better it was by 2001, from the stability of the staff to media relations to the type of players they recruited. It was the rare occasion where the normally self-critical Bennett publicly defended his, and by that time, Soderberg's program.

I will always believe the criticism of Bennett's style started to wear on him, especially the comments after the Final Four loss to Michigan State, a game that was 19–17 at the half. I could hardly blame him. You reach the Final Four only to be popped by some critics who wanted an 85–84 game. That had to sting, so Dick wanted the chance to get a few things off his chest.

Boy, did he ever. He made it clear that he firmly believed that his way was the best way to build the program and that maybe it would be a good idea for people to understand the work that the staff and especially the players put in to make the Badgers a winner.

When he was done, Dick walked off and left the room to a standing ovation. Following him was his lovely wife, Anne, with a grandchild in her arms.

I had an idea of what to expect from Dick, but it was a heck of a speech. It is probably safe to assume that not everyone in the room appreciated the timing of it, but Dick said his piece, and then he moved on. I had the fun task of giving the closing comments. Paul Costanzo started laughing and said, "Good luck following that, buddy!"

All I could do was laugh a little. I'll just say my closing remarks were very brief. I hated to see Brad and his staff go, and I said as much to the crowd. It was uncomfortable because I also had, and always will have, great respect and admiration for Pat Richter. Part of being a high-profile figure is making tough decisions. I think the record shows that most of those decisions, including this one, worked out extremely well for the University of Wisconsin. Pat and his wife, Renee, also happen to be wonderful people, and while I know he did what he thought was in the best interest of the University of Wisconsin, he took no joy in letting someone go.

Richter deserves great credit for taking the high road and not turning that evening into a prolonged verbal mud-wrestling match with a coach he also very much liked and admired. (Still does, I might add.)

There certainly was reason for Dick to keep rooting for the Badgers. Bo hired Tony Bennett as an assistant, where he remained for two seasons before joining Dick at Washington State.

After stepping down from WSU, Dick and Anne moved back to Wisconsin, but his appearances at the Kohl Center have been few and far between. He was back for the 10-year reunion of the Final Four team, and I am hoping he will start to visit more often, be it for games or for any of the numerous off-season public relations events going on with UW athletics. He remains a beloved figure in the history of the program, and that will never change. Nor should it.

As a sports fan, it is easy to sit around with friends and talk about how so-and-so should be fired. Many in the media find it easy to talk and write about the same thing. It started to change for me when I had the chance to be around these people on a daily basis.

You get to know them, and in many cases you get to know their families. Those in my business tend to know just enough to be dangerous, but as a team broadcaster, I get an up-close view of the ups and downs of the coaching profession—the joy of winning a big game and the misery of a tough loss. I have boarded airplanes where the coach has little more than a blank stare, no doubt replaying every moment of a last-second loss.

When Bennett was coaching, he would sit at the front of the aircraft. Mike and I would be a few rows behind him. At times after a loss, we would watch the coach pick up the box score, look at it for a few minutes, and then put it down. He would shake his head. A minute or so later, he would pick up the box score again, maybe hoping something would change. Nothing did, so again he would set aside the paper and shake his head one more time.

For most of us, sport is entertainment—it is certainly not life or death. At the risk of sounding too dramatic—for coaches, it *is* their life. At least it is their livelihood. Those who choose this professional path are big boys and girls, but I would like to believe that in my years of covering athletics, I have gained some appreciation for how hard they work and the sacrifices required of these coaches and their families.

Sometimes changes are necessary. Far more often than not, the moves at the UW have worked out quite well. Call me a softie, but I always find myself rooting for those fired coaches to get another shot. That is why I am happy for guys like Stan Van Gundy. He probably knew all along that one day, he would get fired again. That is just a cold, hard reality about big-time sports, but I have enjoyed watching his playoff teams in the NBA, and I will pull for Brad Soderberg's teams at Lindenwood University in Missouri.

There are enough of those pseudo tough-talking coach killers in the sports media. Unless the coach is a real knucklehead, I tend to err on the side of being too much of a nice guy. I guess I am lucky because the next Badgers head coach I deal with who is jerk will be the first.

14

Rivals

PERHAPS THE MOST APPEALING ASPECT of college sports is the rivalry game. It exists in professional sports with the Yankees–Red Sox. And closer to home, the Brewers and the Cardinals seem to have a nice little feud going.

In pro football, Packers-Bears and Packers-Vikings games always have a little extra spice. Steelers-Ravens games are nasty, too.

However, the college rivalries, especially the football rivalries, last forever. Sure, when one team is winning for a long stretch of time, the special nature of the game can take a hit. But in college football many fans can define a season by how their team fares in the game against the hated opponent.

Through the years, Wisconsin has had two such rivalries—Iowa and Minnesota. From the mid-1970s to the mid-1990s, the series with the Hawkeyes was all Iowa. Adding insult to injury would be the thousands of Iowa fans who invade Camp Randall Stadium, turning the Badgers home field into more of a neutral site. Hawkeyes fans are a loyal bunch, and they travel well. There was a time when Badgers fans stayed away from Camp Randall, opening the door for what some referred to as the "bumble bee" swarm.

Barry Alvarez helped changed that culture, and made the Wisconsin-Iowa series a true rivalry again. One of the more telling moments in the Badgers' turnaround happened in 1998. Wisconsin was en route to a share of the Big Ten championship when it visited Kinnick Stadium in late October. Two years earlier, the Hawkeyes drilled the Badgers 31–0. It was a party in Iowa City and a very long day for Barry and company. The next year Wisconsin ended a two-decade drought and beat the Hawks in Madison 13–10.

By 1998, the Badgers were rolling, and they simply rolled over the Hawkeyes 31–0. It was a dominating performance, and this time thousands of Badgers fans made their way into Iowa's home stadium. At one point late in the game, Iowa was backed up inside its 10-yard line. The south end zone bleachers had a heavy population of fans wearing red, and they were having a ball and yelling very loudly. It got to the point where Iowa had to call a timeout because the offense could not get organized.

You read this correctly. The home team's offense had to take a timeout because of excessive crowd noise, or so it seemed.

In 1999 Iowa was really down, and the Badgers enjoyed one of its most famous days in Camp Randall history. Ron Dayne broke the rushing record, and the Badgers clinched another trip to the Rose Bowl by trouncing the Hawks 41–3. For long-suffering Badgers fans, it was sweet irony that a team that had given Wisconsin so much misery was now on the receiving end of a beat down.

The truth is these teams have taken turns tearing out each other's hearts. In 2005, Iowa ruined Alvarez's last home game as the Badgers head coach. Barry's final team was better than many expected, with heart-stopping victories against Michigan and Minnesota putting the Badgers in position for a January bowl appearance.

For the final game, the school planned a huge postgame ceremony, complete with a highlight video of the Alvarez era, as well as guest speakers such as Pat Richter, Big Ten Commissioner Jim Delany, former UW Chancellor Donna Shalala, and former football star Joe Panos.

Then the Hawkeyes came to town and screwed it up by winning 20–10.

I remember it was my job to serve as the emcee for the postgame ceremony. As the clock was winding down, I felt this major-league headache coming on. The ceremony was on, win or lose, and I knew Barry was not going to be in much of a mood to celebrate.

Not everyone in the stands hung around, but most did. While it was a disappointing day for the Badgers, I thought it would be a good idea to remind everyone how far the program had come in the last 16 years.

Barry, his wife, Cindy, and the entire Alvarez family appreciated the fans' support. While it was not a perfect ending to the home season, I don't think anyone in red wanted Iowa to completely ruin the day.

In 2010, the Badgers had their shot to punch Iowa in the gut. That year's Iowa team was good and had dreams of greatness. In a wild back-and-forth game, the Badgers Montee Ball scored in the final minute to give Wisconsin a 31–30 victory. As big as the win against Ohio State was the previous week, the Badgers rally in Iowa City firmly established Wisconsin as a player on the national stage, and of course it was a key day in the team's run to the Rose Bowl.

The one downside of the new divisional alignment is that the Badgers and the Hawkeyes play in separate divisions, and the rivalry is being interrupted for a couple of years. The all-time series record is 42–42–2—now *that* is a rivalry. With the campuses being a little more than three hours apart, it is a fairly easy commute for fans who like to travel to road games. It will be fun to resume this series.

The longest uninterrupted rivalry in major college football is Wisconsin-Minnesota. I believe it happens to be the most underrated rivalry in the country. We know about Ohio State–Michigan, Texas–Oklahoma, Georgia–Florida, Alabama–Auburn, etc. Those games always get a ton of attention, and rightly so, but I believe the

Badgers-Gophers series has stood the test of time as well as any series in the game.

From a big-picture perspective, this series might not have the BCS ramifications of some of the others, but this is one of those trophy games that gets fans riled up on both sides of the border. There is just something special if your team wins, or galling if it loses, about seeing players take Paul Bunyan's Axe on a victory lap around the field after the game.

In years when the trophy changes hands, the winning team sprints across the field to grab the Axe, which rests by the bench of the school that won the game the previous year. I am pleasantly surprised there has not been a full-scale rumble. Of course, the Badgers have beaten Minnesota eight straight years, so the postgame sprint has been no issue, but no doubt Wisconsin's dominance has the Gopher faithful boiling.

Make no mistake—the Gophers have had their moments. In the 1993 season, the Badgers clearly were the better team. That was Alvarez's first Rose Bowl championship squad. The Gophers were not very good, but on that night, Wisconsin was turnover-prone, fell way behind, and had to scramble just to make the game close. It was the Badgers' only loss of the season.

The games in the Metrodome were incredible. For nearly two decades, just about every game there went down to the wire. Barry's first Big Ten victory was in the dome in 1991 when Wisconsin's Melvin Tucker broke up a pass in the end zone to tight end Patt Evans. In 1995, Aaron Stecker returned a kickoff 100 yards for a score, while John Hall booted a UW record 60-yard field goal. (This is the post-drop-kick era. Pat O'Dea, also known as the "Kangaroo Kicker," popped through a 62-yard drop kick against Northwestern in 1898. Now you know.)

One of my favorite memories from that game was a Jason Maniecki sack late in the fourth quarter. After the game, linebacker Eric Unverzagt told reporters that his message in the huddle to

Maniecki was to "kill everybody." In a football sense, that is pretty much what happened.

No Badger fan will forget the 2005 game. For much different reasons, the same probably can be said of Gophers fans. When Jonathan Casillas blocked a Minnesota punt and Ben Strickland recovered in the end zone in the final half minute, we had a bird's eye view of Gophers fans going through every stage of emotion. Before the punt they were excited because they thought their team was still in position to win the game. They were nervous because the game still was in some doubt. Then they were shocked at the blocked punt and watched in horror as the Badgers scored on the play.

Then they just became ticked off. As we drove home that afternoon, I listened to WCCO's postgame show. It was not pretty. Painful as that kind of loss would be against any team, it hurt even more because it happened against the Badgers.

Leaving the Metrodome, I was careful not to smirk.

At some point, Minnesota's football program will improve, but even with Wisconsin's domination, the rivalry remains strong. It was fairly juicy when Tim Brewster was coaching. Let me just say that Brewster and Bret Bielema did not hit it off very well. Call it a clash of personalities, or perhaps it was just two very competitive men trying to mark their territory, be it in recruiting or any other aspect of trying to win football games.

Their final meeting was in 2010, and Wisconsin won 41–23. With 6:39 remaining in the fourth quarter, James White scored on a 1-yard run, giving the Badgers a 41–16 lead. Bielema went for two, and after the game Brewster made it clear he did not appreciate it.

The decision reminded me of the 1968 Ohio State–Michigan game when the Buckeyes blitzed Michigan 50–14. After the final OSU touchdown, Hayes ordered a two-point conversion try. After the game when a media member asked Hayes why he went for two, the coach reportedly replied, "Because I couldn't go for three!"

Like it or not, Bielema has said if the shoe was on the other foot, he would expect the opponent to go for two, as well. In my book, as long as one is consistent with his thinking, then I suppose going for two late in the fourth quarter is fair game.

If nothing else, it gives talk show hosts something to gab about for a few days.

The rivalries with Iowa and Minnesota are long running, and the series records are very close. One that is not so close but has picked up a ton of steam in recent years is Wisconsin–Ohio State.

I suppose beating a team that is ranked No. 1 in both football and basketball can do something to stir the emotions of both fan bases. OSU leads the all-time series 54–18–5, but in the last 30 years this is a much closer deal, with the Buckeyes only holding a 15–11–1 edge.

In 1999, 2001, and 2004, the Badgers won in the Horseshoe. Ohio State won in Madison in 2000 and in 2002. On a couple of occasions, some players on the winning team gathered at midfield and did a little dance, either on OSU's "Block O" or on the Badgers' "Motion W." It might not have been a real big deal, but it was enough to give people something to talk about.

After the 2004 game, in which Wisconsin was clearly the better team and proved it, a little scrap broke out. From the booth, I was afraid the Badgers would lose a couple of players for the following week's game at Purdue, but cooler heads prevailed. It was mostly pushing and shoving, with big Joe Thomas in the middle of it all. I had to smile when I saw the Badgers massive left tackle in the fray. Nobody was going to hurt that guy.

Clearly the Badgers program has grown to the point where there is no fear of facing such a perennial power. I have long believed Wisconsin's rise has gotten under the skin of those in Buckeye Nation, who no doubt prefer the good old days when Ohio State and Michigan rode roughshod against the rest of the league, then settled the Big Ten title with their season-ending tilt.

In 2011, several folks from Columbus told me the home game everyone wanted to see was against Wisconsin. Yes, Michigan is still the biggest of the big games, but those little ol' Badgers have become a team that fans in Ohio are learning to hate.

I believe it. As the team buses made their way from the hotel to Ohio Stadium, the route took them through the north side of campus. Hundreds of fans were lined up along the street, and when they realized these were the Wisconsin team buses, they started flipping the bird, shooting the moon, and shouting all kinds of obscenities. Other than that, those Buckeyes fans gave the Badgers a warm welcome.

The game was a heartbreaker for Wisconsin. The Badgers had rallied from a 12-point fourth-quarter deficit to take the lead with a little more than a minute to play. However, Ohio State quarterback Braxton Miller fired a 40-yard touchdown pass with 20 seconds to play, giving OSU a dramatic victory.

How dramatic was it? The fans in Columbus stormed the field. Maybe it has happened before, but other than a game that clinched a title, I cannot remember Ohio State fans rushing the field after a game against any team other than Michigan.

That is a good indication of how far the UW program has grown.

Let the rivalry resume this fall.

15
Rivals, Part Two

"I'LL REMEMBER THAT."

Those were the words of Michigan State coach Tom Izzo directed to Wisconsin's Bo Ryan during the postgame handshake on February 11, 2003. In the closing seconds of the Badgers 64–53 victory, Devin Harris dribbled out of traffic to the front court, and then set up a perfect lob for the high-flying Alando Tucker, who ended the game with a resounding dunk.

As the clock struck zero, I turned to look at Izzo, who was none too happy, and he let Bo know it with that simple line. At the time, all I could think of was "Well, it's on now." The previous year the Badgers stopped Michigan State's home winning streak at 53 games. Now Wisconsin beat the Spartans again with a game-ending flush for good measure.

This was unfamiliar territory for MSU, which was not far removed from three straight trips to the Final Four, including winning it all in 2000. That season, Michigan State defeated Wisconsin four times, twice in the regular season, then in the Big Ten Tournament and one more time in the National Semifinal game in Indianapolis.

After the game in 2003, Izzo was steamed. Later, so was Bo. Plenty was written and said about the dunk in the closing seconds, including some words from national pundits who questioned why anyone would do such a thing.

It became a bit humorous. Here is some breaking news— Wisconsin did not invent the late-game slam. Michigan State has done it a time or two, including a game a few years earlier against in-state rival Michigan. In the final minute, Jason Richardson was on the receiving end of a lob pass that he turned into an impressive dunk. That particular play helped close out a 114–63 squeaker against the Wolverines.

For his part, Harris said after the game that if he had to do it over, he would not have thrown the pass. It is a simple case of making a mountain out of a molehill, but it sure did turn up this rivalry a notch.

Keep in mind, you do not hear Bo Ryan talk about rivalries. He is as good as any coach I have been around in just playing the next game. That might sound dull, but it has worked rather well for his teams.

Fans look at it a bit differently. The February 2003 game was the only meeting between the two teams that season, but the following year they met three times with the Badgers winning all three. Two of those games were gut busters for Michigan State. The March 2, 2004, matchup was the Banner Night game when the Badgers, as well as ESPN's production crew, spotted a rolled-up banner hanging from the Breslin Center rafters. Michigan State was playing for at least a share of the Big Ten title that night, and plans were in place for a postgame ceremony.

Only the ceremony never happened. Late in regulation, Harris nailed a long three to tie the game. Then with 22 seconds remaining in regulation time, MSU's Chris Hill, a good free throw shooter, missed a pair from the line and the game went into overtime. In the final minute of OT, Clayton Hanson stuck a huge three, giving the Badgers a 62–58 lead. They also were clutch at the foul line, hitting 9-of-10 in the extra session.

To be fair, the Spartans missed big man Paul Davis, who was having quite a night with 25 points and 10 rebounds before being sidelined with leg cramps.

It was quite the night for the Badgers. I said on the air that they crashed the party in East Lansing, Michigan. To say Izzo is a great coach is very much an understatement. He also is one who wears his emotions on his sleeves, and as he walked off the floor that night, he had the look of someone who ran over his dog. It was setting up perfectly—he could have beaten a nemesis and collected another trophy, but the Badgers denied him that opportunity.

The teams later met in Indianapolis for the Big Ten Tournament. In the semi-finals, the Badgers struck again. It was a back-and-forth game at Conseco Fieldhouse with neither team leading by more than five points in the second half.

As time was winding down, Harris drilled a three, then Mike Wilkinson made a couple of free throws to give the Badgers a 67–66 lead. MSU's Kelvin Torbert misfired on a jumper, and Wisconsin's Zach Morley grabbed the rebound. After being fouled, Morley split his free throws, giving the Spartans one final chance, but a Maurice Ager jumper was off the mark and Wisconsin got past Michigan State once again.

The Spartans have dished out some pain, as well. In 2007, the Badgers went into the Breslin Center ranked No. 1 in the nation. In basketball, rankings only mean so much, but that was pretty heady stuff for the Badgers and their fans. Sparty was ready, and as the second half unfolded, Michigan State started to pull away.

Marcus Landry did what he could to keep the Badgers close, scoring the first nine points of the second half. However, after Landry hit his fourth three-pointer of the night to give Wisconsin a 47–43 lead, the Spartans went on a 21–6 run led by guard Drew Neitzel, who scored 28 points on the night.

In the final minute of the game, Izzo called a timeout. I thought he was going to substitute some players, but I don't believe he did. It was just a chance for the fans to soak up the atmosphere, and did they ever.

After the game, the MSU students stormed the floor, which was innocent enough. Then things started to get a little more interesting.

As is often the case after games, the TV crew will either tape or conduct a live interview with the winning coach and perhaps a player. In this case, ESPN's Erin Andrews was taping an interview with Neitzel. For whatever reason, the crew chose to do the interview right by our radio location. Why, I have no idea, but all of a sudden fans were swarming by our table to get on camera. Some of them started to jostle us. They were not being jerks—they were just excited fans who wanted to surround their hero, Drew Neitzel, but they began bumping me and my producer, who happens to live in Michigan. Eventually I had to raise my arms to hold people off, and I gave a little push to a man who was trying to get closer to Neitzel.

At that point, I was getting pretty annoyed. Then the man said, "Hey, do you mind? That's my son!" Yes, I gave a slight shove to Drew Neitzel's father. I went from being upset to feeling like a dope. I shook his hand and waved him through, but I still say the security was a little weak.

Actually, they do a very good job there. I think I was more upset at ESPN for choosing to do an interview right next to the visiting radio position, but somehow I don't think anyone from the world-wide leader really cared about our broadcast.

The truth is I always look forward to those games with Michigan State. As much as Wisconsin fans love to razz Izzo, his coaching record speaks for itself. I cannot say I know him well, but he always has been friendly enough. We have a mutual friend in former Wisconsin football standout Bob Landsee who, like Izzo, is from Upper Michigan, or as they would say, they are fellow Youppers

As for the Bo vs. Izzo thing, there are those from both sides who say these two men are more alike than either might be willing to admit. Who knows? Maybe one day when they are done trying to beat each other, they can sit down, have a few beers, and tell stories about some of the great Wisconsin–Michigan State games. It sure would be enjoyable to sit in on that conversation.

• • •

For Badger fans, the Michigan State game is the annual must-see Big Ten game. Out of conference, the answer is easy—Marquette.

This might get me in trouble with Badgers fans, but there are times when I believe there is more atmosphere when the teams play in Milwaukee. Clearly, it is a game that Golden Eagles fans circle, and perhaps because the school has no football program, there is little question that basketball is king.

A few years ago the Badgers played Marquette at the Bradley Center. It was a Saturday afternoon game on national television. Mike Lucas, our engineer, Dave McCann, and I arrived about three hours or so before tip-off. The student section was packed, and everyone was watching the motion picture *Dumb and Dumber*. It was classic—not the movie, just the fact that the students would get there so early.

It did not take me very long to understand the sometimes deep-seeded dislike the fan bases can have for one another. Marquette fans can view the UW as that small-town liberal school, while Badgers fans will claim Marquette is a big-time wannabe that can't decide on a school nickname.

The reality is both schools are excellent (I really mean this!). I have friends who are proud alums of both Marquette and Wisconsin.

In the late 1980s and early '90s, Marquette fans, in an effort to have some fun with the UW football program's woes, would break into a chant of "Bad-ger Foot-ball." Obviously, that chant no longer has the same effect.

There were years when these teams met a couple of times each season, and sometimes during the middle of Big Ten play—1990 was one of those years. Steve Yoder was not very thrilled with the idea of stepping out of conference in February, but his counterpart, Kevin O'Neill, seemed to embrace the idea. O'Neill is a piece of work, and on the night of February 19, 1990, his personality was on full display.

To make a long story short, the Badgers beat Marquette 82–65. The individual standout was Marquette's Tony Smith. Wisconsin could not guard him. Smith scored 44 points, but fortunately for the Badgers, nobody else really hurt them. Smith's night would have been a bigger story, except for two things—his team lost, and his coach got himself thrown out of the game. On his way to the UW Field House visiting locker room, O'Neill stopped by the Wisconsin bench and shook everyone's hand, one by one. It was quite the sight. O'Neill went off on the officials, and then he went into political candidate mode. It was pretty funny stuff.

In recent years, there has been some added spice to this series. For one thing, both programs are good, and that is good for college basketball in this state. Wisconsin-Marquette games always have meaning to fans in this state, but when both are Top 25 teams, and fans across the country can catch the games on ESPN, it's a great showcase for the sport in Wisconsin.

Another factor in this rivalry being ramped up is that you have talented players from Madison who chose Marquette, while others from Milwaukee who opted to attend UW. Wesley Matthews and Vander Blue are two examples of Madison athletes who believed it was better for them to be Golden Eagles. Devin Harris and Marcus Landry are recent Milwaukee-area players who moved about 80 miles west.

The Blue decision really stirred emotions from both sides. At first, the former Memorial High School star gave a verbal commitment to Wisconsin. Then he reconsidered and decided Marquette was a better fit. Naturally, there were hard feelings with some Badgers fans to the point where it was getting more than a little silly. My philosophy is simple: if a player does not want to be at Wisconsin, go somewhere else. Do you really want someone in your program who is unhappy?

When the Badgers played at Marquette in December 2010, the game program at the Bradley Center featured—take a guess— Vander Blue. It was just another little tweak between the two rivals.

On that day, the Badgers had the last laugh as they beat Marquette 69–64. A key play was turned in by freshman guard Josh Gasser from Port Washington, a town north of Milwaukee. He helped force a turnover in the closing seconds that clinched the game for Bo Ryan's team. The following year, the Golden Eagles returned the favor with a victory at the Kohl Center.

Coaching staff personalities can help make a rivalry special. For long time college fans in this state, the great Al McGuire was a rather polarizing figure, which helps explain one of the more infamous photographs in either school's basketball history.

In February 1974, Marquette beat the Badgers on a last-second shot by Maurice Lucas. McGuire jumped onto the scorer's table at Milwaukee Arena. It was then that Glenn Hughes, the father of Badgers twin brothers Kim and Kerry Hughes, stood up and delivered a one-finger salute.

In the foreground of the photograph is Wisconsin coach John Powless walking off the floor. For better or worse, you could say that photo symbolizes the feelings these two fan bases have for one another.

Gotta love those in-state games.

• • •

Similar to football, the Wisconsin–Ohio State basketball rivalry has gathered some steam in recent years. Bo Ryan and Thad Matta get along, so there is no juicy element between the coaches. This rivalry is more of a product of how good both programs have been, but I think it is safe to say that the fans do not get along quite as well as the opposing coaches.

It will be interesting to see how this rivalry stands the test of time. With any luck, the series will continue to produce high-stakes games. Whatever the case, showcase games such as Michigan State, Marquette, and at times Ohio State, add a little heat to a long, cold winter.

Maybe for a casual fan, college basketball does not really start until March Madness. Those who believe that are missing some great games in December, January, and February. Spend one night in an arena where these rivals go at it, and your opinion might change.

16

"Stupid Is As Stupid Does"

WHEN YOU ARE THE PLAY-BY-PLAY ANNOUNCER for a school, your duties can go far beyond calling a game and shouting, "Touchdown Wisconsin!" on Saturday afternoons.

When talking to younger broadcasters, I try to emphasize the importance not only of being able to describe a game but also to be ready and willing to speak in front of groups of all sizes and backgrounds. Those groups can be made up of very wealthy individuals who donate large sums of money to an athletic department. They also can be made up of folks who might not have the disposable income to afford a ticket, but they love their team and make a point to watch and/or listen to every game.

The radio voice of a team often serves as the emcee to any number of functions during the year. Some announcers have carved quite a niche just in that area alone. In our state, Milwaukee Brewers broadcaster Bob Uecker can have audiences doubled over in laughter. The late Green Bay Packers/Milwaukee Bucks/ Wisconsin Badgers voice Jim Irwin was known for his sharp wit. People tell me when Jim was at the microphone, any banquet could turn into a roast.

The late Jack Buck, who called St. Louis Cardinals games for years in addition to his network TV duties, also was considered a

149

superb speaker. No doubt the late Harry Caray had people rolling in the aisles, as well.

Me? Well, since I am speaking to college fans, alums, and donors, I tend to play it safe most of the time. Madison, Wisconsin, is known for many things, including its politically correct nature, so I generally err on the side of caution. Besides, with many of the events I emcee, it is quite clear that I am not exactly the main attraction. People want to hear what Barry Alvarez, Bo Ryan, Bret Bielema, or any of the other coaches have to say. I generally let them be the funny guys.

One of the really enjoyable aspects to being an emcee is having the opportunity to meet some of the true movers and shakers in sports and other walks of life. The day before the Wisconsin football team hosted Nebraska in the 2011 Big Ten opener, there was a luncheon on campus. Part of the program included yours truly conducting a little question-and-answer session with Hall of Fame coaches Barry Alvarez and Tom Osborne. Since the game marked Nebraska's Big Ten Conference debut, the entire week was a very big deal. So was the luncheon.

I had never met Osborne, but anybody with any knowledge of college football knows how incredibly successful he was as the Cornhuskers coach. He led the team with a low-key but very effective style, winning three national titles in the 1990s. When I told my wife, Linda, that I would be emceeing this event, she asked, "Sometimes do you feel like you are Forrest Gump?"

What she means is that I have been lucky enough to be in the company of some pretty well-known and highly successful people. In the movie, the character played by Tom Hanks finds himself in the same room as historical figures such as Presidents Lyndon Johnson and Richard Nixon, Elvis, John Lennon, and Abbie Hoffman. Hopefully now Linda's comment makes more sense.

I am still waiting to introduce a president, but I have had my fair share of chats with governors, congressmen, multi-millionaire businessmen, not to mention some of the more famous sports stars of the last generation.

The luncheon with Alvarez and Osborne was a real treat. The room was packed with nearly 500 people, most of whom are very loyal donors to the university. The entire week was hectic but very special to Alvarez. A Nebraska alum, Alvarez led the Huskers in tackles in 1967. The previous year, the former linebacker had two stops in a game against Wisconsin at Camp Randall. He also intercepted a pass and returned it 25 yards. Alvarez has received more grief about that play than you can imagine.

Barry was known as a tough player, but by his own admission he was slow. Actually, some might say he could not run a lick. Alvarez often describes how an announcer might call his interception return.

"Alvarez is at the 50...he's at the 49...the 48," etc. He has told the story hundreds of times, including in his own book, *Don't Flinch*.

To his credit, about a week before the luncheon, he asked me to have the UW video folks dig up that old highlight clip. "You really want to get razzed about that again?" I asked. He thought it would be fun, and he was right.

In a show of mercy for Alvarez, Osborne chose not to dissect Alvarez's lack of speed, but he did tell a story that left the crowd laughing. Keep in mind that Osborne is a soft-spoken man, very even-keeled. With that image, now picture him as he describes Alvarez the player. "Barry got hurt a lot at Nebraska," Osborne told the luncheon crowd, adding that in one game Osborne asked Alvarez what was wrong.

"When I push here, I get this terrible pain," Alvarez said while pointing to his head. He pointed to his neck and said, "When I push here, the pain is awful." Then Alvarez pointed to his chest and claimed, "And when I push here, the pain is excruciating."

Osborne, now with a smirk on his face, continued, "So we got Barry on a stretcher and called an ambulance. They found out what he had—a broken finger."

The crowd, including Barry, broke out in laughter.

• • •

In 2001, the Badgers opened the football season by playing Virginia in the Eddie Robinson Classic, named after the longtime coach at Grambling State University. Longtime indeed, as Robinson was the coach at that institution from 1941 through the 1997 season. He died in 2007 of Alzheimer's, and while he looked frail at that 2001 luncheon, I recall we had a very pleasant conversation about college football, and he mentioned how impressed he was with Wisconsin's program.

Eddie Robinson was a true gentleman, and sitting next to such an historical figure is something I will forever cherish. In my line of work, it is easy to become a tad jaded, but all cynicism went away when I had the chance to meet Coach Robinson.

A non-UW event that I always look forward to attending is the annual NFL Alumni banquet in Madison. Through the years, this function has generated more than $1.7 million for a variety of Madison-area organizations, including the Boy Scouts of America, Lad Lake, and the American Family Children's Hospital.

Former Badger football players Bob Landsee and Joe Armentrout are among those who do a lot of heavy lifting to make this event such a success. They have been kind enough to ask me to emcee their banquet, and through the years those in attendance have had the chance to hear from guest speakers such as Hank Stram, Bart Starr, Jerry Kramer, Dan Hampton, and many other NFL legends.

Stram, who died in 2005, is perhaps best known for allowing NFL Films to wire him for sound in Super Bowl IV. "Just keep matriculating the ball down the field, boys," as well as his famous play call of "65 Toss Power Trap," remain well-known lines some 40 years after his Kansas City Chiefs beat the Minnesota Vikings in the final Super Bowl featuring the old NFL vs. AFL champions.

Being in Wisconsin, fans still love hearing about the Lombardi-era Packers. Sometimes I wonder how those guys can keep telling the same stories, but then again, why not? I must admit, I still enjoy listening to them. When Jerry Kramer was the guest speaker, we talked about that brutally cold day at Yankee Stadium when the Packers beat the New York Giants in the 1962 NFL title game. A guard, Kramer also handled place kicks, and with the wind gusting to 40 mph, he booted three field goals to help Green Bay win the championship.

For his efforts, he was awarded a game ball. Linebacker Ray Nitschke won MVP honors for which he received a Corvette. As Kramer likes to crack, "That is what a lineman's life is like."

While Bart Starr's coaching career did not work out as Packers fans had hoped, the quarterback always will be a revered figure, as well he should be. I found him to be quite humble. The year he was the guest speaker, the folks running the banquet program wanted to run a highlight video. Starr wanted none of it. He thought it was too much about him and not about the team. For a time, he was adamant about not showing the video.

I had to work on him for a while. Here I am—Johnny Nobody trying to talk a Hall of Famer into letting us run a video of Starr's career. Finally, I said, "Bart, these people love you. They can't get enough of hearing about you and your team, and it never gets old for Packers fans to watch highlights from those days."

Finally he gave in, and we enjoyed the video. Then Starr took the stage and told the old Lombardi stories one more time. Maybe many in the room had heard them before, but after all these years there remains something larger than life about those 1960s Green Bay Packers teams. The room was his, and the ovation was genuine.

Even though I have served as an emcee countless times, I would be lying if I told you that I never get nervous. I certainly had some butterflies before a function in New York City in December 2010. When Barry Alvarez was inducted into the College Football Hall of Fame, there was a reception the night before in a modest-sized room at a restaurant in the heart of the city. It included some of

Barry's closest friends in and out of the coaching business as well as some of the more high-powered figures in college athletics.

Those in the room included Oklahoma football coach Bob Stoops, South Carolina's Steve Spurrier, former Iowa coach Hayden Fry, and Hall of Famer Lou Holtz. Others who attended the reception were several of Barry's former players, a few fellow athletics directors, Big Ten commissioner Jim Delany, and BTN president Mark Silverman. That is just to name a few—for college athletics, it truly was "Power Alley."

My goal was simple—do not screw it up. The beauty of hosting a program such as this is knowing that I just need to do the introductions and then get the heck out of the way. It was a terrific night. When talking about what Barry meant to him as a player and as a young man, former UW quarterback Brooks Bollinger became emotional. Holtz broke up the crowd, saying it is great to honor someone who is so successful—then quipped, "But enough about me."

Seeing former players such as Bollinger, Tarek Saleh, Don Davey, Jim Sorgi, and others, not to mention the man who hired Barry, Pat Richter, in a room together, made me stop and think about how far this program has come in the last two decades. In 1990, the thought of honoring someone for having such success leading Wisconsin's football program was nothing more than a dream—probably an impossible dream. Yet here we were, on a chilly December evening in New York with other great coaches in the room, celebrating the success that is Wisconsin football.

And here was some radio announcer, who had nothing at all to do with any of that success, enjoying the view and visiting with the many important people who have helped make the games we watch so much fun.

At functions such as these, my goal is simply to do my job as best I can and move the program along at a comfortable pace. It is later when I realize how special so many of these events can be.

As I have said many times—it sure beats working.

17
The Assistants

THE PERSONALITIES AND THE TEACHING STYLES CAN VARY. You have the quieter, more flat-line coaches who want players to be self-starters. Then you have those who begin the day with an extra dose of Red Bull and/or Starbucks and go 100 mph. They are the assistant coaches, and behind every successful head man is a group of assistants who work 18 hour days trying to figure out how to win the next game.

These are the men who look at video for hours on end, determining the strengths and weaknesses of the upcoming opponent. They also study video of their own team, looking at what is working, what is not working, and why. The assistant coach spends countless hours on the recruiting trail, often in small town America, hoping to find the next star player.

It is true that assistants at major schools such as Wisconsin can make pretty good money, especially compared to even 15 or 20 years ago, but this line of work is a lifestyle decision that a family needs to understand. During the season, Daddy will not be around very much. I have known assistants who have said—only half jokingly—that at the end of July they kiss the wife and kids goodbye and say, "I'll see you in a few months."

They do not look for sympathy. They simply are explaining what the job requires.

Through the years, the Badgers have been fortunate to have many outstanding assistant coaches, several of whom have gone on to run their own programs. It has been interesting getting to know many of these coaches and learning their philosophies. I have to admit to at least some surprise that some became head coaches, but it certainly has led me to follow teams I otherwise would have had little interest in watching.

It is worth noting that even in some of Wisconsin football's darkest days, a few assistants went on to win a lot of games elsewhere. From 1987–88, Craig Bohl was a UW assistant under Don Morton. After leaving Madison, his stops included a highly successful run as a Nebraska assistant, and for the last nine years Bohl has been the head coach at North Dakota State, where he led the Bison to the 2011 FCS national championship.

Also on Morton's staff was Bob Babich, who served as an assistant in 1988–89. For the last seven years, Babich has been with the Chicago Bears. He was head coach Lovie Smith's first hire. Smith was a UW assistant in 1987.

The Alvarez coaching tree includes Bill Callahan, Dan McCarney, Rob Ianello, and Brad Childress. Of those, Childress probably enjoyed the most success. I use the word "enjoyed" with some hesitation, which I will explain shortly.

Childress coached the Minnesota Vikings from 2006 through the tenth game of 2010. In 2008 and 2009, his team won the NFC North. The '09 team was terrific, led by quarterback Brett Favre. The Vikings rolled through the regular season with a 12–4 record, which included two victories against the Green Bay Packers in very emotionally charged games. In November 2009, the team extended Childress' contract through 2013. Everything seemed to be in place for a long run with the Purple and Gold.

Then along came the NFC Championship Game in New Orleans. For Packers fans, this was unfolding as a worst-case scenario. Favre left Green Bay in very controversial fashion. He spent a year with the New York Jets and then ended up playing for the Packers' hated rival to the west. Favre was on the brink of taking the Vikings to the Super Bowl. As the fourth quarter was winding down, the Vikings were driving into field goal range.

Then it happened. Favre threw an interception. The Saints eventually won in overtime. From there, the world went south on Childress, Favre, and the Vikings franchise. The following year, the Vikings floundered. With their record at 3–7, and Favre finally breaking down physically, the team fired Childress.

In some ways similar to Stan Van Gundy, Brad Childress is one reason why it is important not to judge a book by its cover. I always liked Chilly. I consider him a bright, loyal family man. He also is incredibly intense, and all too often the public did not get much of a chance to see the more human side of him.

Even as a Wisconsin assistant, Childress was tightly wound during the season. That is just his nature, and it is what makes him tick in a highly competitive business. Always cooperative with me, he was all business. I knew that most of the time when we did an interview, there would be little in the way of small talk, and that was okay.

Out of season, or even in-season after a UW victory, we would see a much more relaxed Brad Childress. His brother is quite the chef, and among his talents is the ability to make killer barbeque ribs. Sometimes following a game, and at times during the summer, there would be a rib fest at the Childress household. Nobody left hungry.

• • •

Bill Callahan is another former Badgers assistant who saw the good and the bad of being a head coach. Under Alvarez, Callahan was the offensive line coach. I have never met a laid-back O-line coach, and that includes Callahan. At the risk of being really repetitive, I never had any issues with Bill. What I will say is whenever we had a conversation, he seemed to have this distant look in his eyes. I am guessing he had about a thousand things on his mind, and chatting with me was not one of them.

Callahan was the Oakland Raiders head coach in the Super Bowl season of 2002. One year later he was out of a job. He ended up as Nebraska's head coach, and his run in Lincoln was anything put pretty. After Nebraska, Callahan became the New York Jets offensive line coach, where star center Nick Mangold told the *New York Times*, "He's [Callahan] at such an advanced level in knowledge of the game, but he has an uncanny ability to translate it down to us normal people."

There have been many strong personalities on the UW football staff. Defensive line coach John Palermo and offensive line coach Jim Hueber come to mind. It also is clear that almost everyone they coached speaks of those two in glowing terms.

Palermo could be as tough as any coach I have ever seen. He also could be pretty funny. J.P. could just unload on a player, then turn around and give him a little wink. For the most part, I figured those guys on the defensive line understood where Palermo was coming from, and more often than not that position group was very good and sometimes great.

He might not like this, but I tend to believe that Palermo's bark is worse than his bite. Actually, others have told me the same thing. Over time, perhaps he and Barry Alvarez grew apart, but when the program was rolling in the 1990s, those guys made quite a combo.

• • •

A good friend of Palermo's is Jim Hueber, who also is an old-school tough guy. He came to Wisconsin as the running backs coach, and then he moved to the offensive line after Callahan left. Much like J.P., Huebs could verbally undress a player with the best of them, and he could also be a challenging interview, but if you can get through that part, you understand how he became such a good coach. Just take a look at some of Wisconsin's offensive lines, including that cast of characters in the late 1990s such as Chris McIntosh, Aaron Gibson, Mark Tauscher, Casey Rabach, Bill Ferrario, and Dave Costa. They just dominated people, and in many ways made up the heart and soul of those championship teams.

I actually believe Hueber would make a good broadcaster. When he was in Madison, I would do weekly interviews with him in his office. I would stop by on Thursday mornings, and we taped a little five-minute show to run during our local pregame programming. He can tell a good story—at Wisconsin he was the team historian on the Wisconsin-Minnesota rivalry. However, Hueber can put the sportscasting career on hold. After being out of coaching in 2011, Jim is back in the game as an assistant at the University of Pittsburgh under Paul Chryst.

• • •

Speaking of Chryst, he is one of my favorite assistants, and in the fall of 2012 he will begin his first season as a head coach. When I first arrived in Madison in 1988, Chryst was a tight end on a bad Wisconsin team. In the last several years, he became one of college football's most respected offensive coordinators. At Wisconsin, Chryst directed a group that put up record statistics. True to form, he never took much credit. He would just say that he hopes he "doesn't screw it up."

I especially appreciate his dry sense of humor. In 2010, there were some who criticized the Badgers for scoring 70-plus points on three occasions, including an 83–20 rout of Indiana. To be honest, on that day the only way Wisconsin would not score is if the quarterback took a knee on every snap. Anyway, one day after practice when reporters asked Chryst about the high point totals, he simply said, "On offense, the object is to score."

Nobody cuts through the B.S. better than Paul Chryst.

He is probably like any number of assistants, but what really stands out to me is how much he seems to enjoy the process of preparation. I think he truly loves looking at all that video and finding ways to exploit an opposing defense. He loves practice. I mean he *really* loves practice.

I also have never heard him say, "We gotta *win* this game." Chryst focuses on doing everything you can to be ready for a game. From there, he will say the result will take care of itself.

Not to sound like his agent, but getting to know Paul Chryst the coach has helped me define the word passion. To many, passion can mean how animated you are, how much you shout, pump your fist, whatever. Make no mistake, Chryst can raise his voice on the practice field, but for the most part, he is more flat line than most, save for a tongue-in-cheek wise guy remark. Do not confuse that with lack of passion. The man is a stickler for preparation. To me, that defines passion. What are you doing to make yourself better when very few are watching? Anyone can thump his chest and wave a towel when 80,000 fans are screaming. It is what you do when the seats are empty that can define your level of passion.

Like so many of Wisconsin's assistant coaches, Chryst does not need a packed stadium and blaring music to enjoy his work. He just loves football, and Wisconsin was lucky to have him.

• • •

The Wisconsin coaching tree exists in basketball, as well. Former Badger assistants who became head coaches include Ray McCallum, Stan Van Gundy, Sean Miller, Tony Bennett, Rob Jeter, Saul Phillips, and Howard Moore.

When considering the rise of Wisconsin basketball, McCallum played an important role with his recruiting skills, helping bring in players such as Tracy Webster, Michael Finley, and Rashard Griffith. For younger or other newer Badger fans, perhaps the name Ray McCallum is less familiar than others. He first joined Steve

Yoder's UW staff in 1984 when Wisconsin basketball was struggling for attention. As the program improved by the early 1990s, Stu Jackson's presence could overshadow the rest of the staff. Yet in a rather understated way, McCallum's work was crucial in getting the program on the national map.

Looking back, it is easy to say that Stu Jackson had plenty of help with his first coaching staff, which was made up of McCallum, Van Gundy, and Miller. That is quite a collection of basketball coaching talent. The next year was not too shabby either, with McCallum, Bob Beyer, and Tim Buckley.

Beyer has had an interesting coaching ride, working for men such as Jackson, Bob Knight, Kevin O'Neill, and then Van Gundy with the Orlando Magic. Heck, Beyer could write a best-selling book about working with that crew!

Buckley is one of those people who never seems to have a bad day. He has been a head coach at Ball State, where his team made a splash at the 2001 Maui Invitational with upset wins against Kansas and UCLA. Assistant coaching stops beyond Wisconsin include a stint at Iowa under Steve Alford and at Marquette and Indiana under Tom Crean. T-Buck has been part of some difficult rebuilding jobs, but his upbeat nature is something I have always admired.

Tony Bennett's more laid-back style is in direct contrast to his father, Dick Bennett. As Tony likes to say, "I'm more like my mother, while Kathi takes after my dad." Kathi is the women's basketball coach at Northern Illinois. Earlier in her career, she led UW–Oshkosh to the Division III national title, and she also led the programs at Evansville and Indiana. In addition, Kathi was a terrific assistant coach at Wisconsin. Much like her father's teams, the defense improved when Kathi joined the staff.

After Dick stepped down as Washington State's head coach, making way for Tony to take the job, I could not help but laugh when catching a Cougars game on TV. Dick would be in the stands, and the TV producers would love to point a camera on the elder Bennett, who would have this look of agony on his face. Meanwhile Tony appeared perfectly calm on the bench. Different strokes for different folks.

I always thought Rob Jeter just *looked* like a head coach. A personal favorite of Bo Ryan's, Jeter did a great job in Bo's early days as the Badgers' head man. Rob made sure the players understood the message Bo was trying to send. As competitive as Ryan is, I tend to believe he does not enjoy those games with Milwaukee, but the Badgers coach is a staunch believer in playing the state's other Division I programs.

Saul Phillips was Bo's director of basketball operations before becoming an assistant coach, then a head coach, at North Dakota State. As a head man, he led the Bison to its first Division I NCAA Tournament bid. As an assistant at NDSU, he watched his team pull a stunner at Wisconsin's expense, beating the Badgers at the Kohl Center in January 2006.

Normally Bo would want nothing to do with scheduling a non-conference game in the middle of the Big Ten season. He made an exception in this case, and it turned into one of the bigger surprises of that season in college basketball. It was a strange day. The Badgers shot just 22 percent from the floor, while the Bison hit 23-of-46 shots. It was the perfect storm, and as lousy as I felt for the home team, I could not help but feel good for Salty.

After the game I sent him a message, demanding another game. Phillips gave me the old line from the movie *Rocky* when Rocky Balboa told Apollo Creed that he did not want a rematch. "Don't want one," the Italian Stallion said.

In the past 25 years, one of the more universally liked assistants has been Howard Moore, who became the head man at Illinois-Chicago in 2010. A former Badger player, Howard played limited minutes in his career, but he is another person I would put on my list of favorite people. He played for three different coaches, and in such circumstances it might be easy to put in your time and then move on from a school and never look back.

That is not how Howard Moore rolls. He joined Bo Ryan's staff in 2005–06. In addition to his work for Bo, Howard thought it was important to reach out to some of his teammates who might have lost touch with the program. He remains good friends with guys like Michael Finley, Rashard Griffith, and a number of others. By reaching out to those former players, Moore's efforts went a long way in helping the UW maintain a good relationship with some Badgers of yesteryear.

I believe next on the list of future successful head coaches is Greg Gard, who has been an assistant under Ryan since the UW–Platteville days dating back to 1993. A tireless worker, Gard is like Paul Chryst in that both men are lousy self-promoters. They just love the game and would prefer that their work speaks for itself.

Some people see Gardo and get the impression he is a quiet, stand-off-to-the-side kind of person. Those people are missing the boat. He will talk your ear off, and it is clear he is an excellent recruiter. When you are the one who targets some of those Minnesota standouts such as Jordan Taylor and Jon Leuer, just to name two, you must be doing something right.

When searching for coaches, athletic directors sometimes outsmart themselves. Both Gard and fellow assistant Gary Close have interviewed for head coaching positions, but maybe because these men lack the so-called flashy demeanor of others, those schools go in another direction.

I am just a broadcaster, but it seems to me that some schools just need a ball coach, not someone who is really good at the Midnight Madness event in October. Coaches like Gard and Close can have as much fun as the next guy. They just go about their business in a more under-the-radar manner. Since Wisconsin has been so good for so long, it surprises me that more schools have not gone after them.

Then again, other schools' losses have been Wisconsin's gain.

18
Football Venues

A POPULAR QUESTION PEOPLE WILL ASK is what other Big Ten cities have an atmosphere similar to Wisconsin?

The answer varies from football to basketball. For instance, Penn State's Beaver Stadium is top notch for football, but the basketball crowds at the Bryce Jordan Center are often pretty small. Those who show up are vocal, but many years the empty seats outnumber the occupied seats.

Keeping in the spirit of lists, here are some of my favorite spots. Keep in mind I have yet to make a trip to Lincoln, Nebraska, for a football game, and the basketball trip in 2011 was right after Christmas with the students gone for the semester break, making it unfair to judge the Cornhuskers just yet.

1. Beaver Stadium—Penn State University. Clearly the program is entering a new era. Joe Paterno passed away last January. The allegations involving former assistant coach Jerry Sandusky stirred the entire range of human emotions. As of this writing, the Sandusky story is far from done, so for the purposes of this chapter, we will keep our attention on the stadiums in general and what I have experienced through the years.

The bad news is State College, Pennsylvania, is in the middle of the state and can be a difficult commute for many fans in

Wisconsin. Still, if you can make it there, by all means give it a try. Those people are tailgating professionals. Clearly, this is an area that lives for football, and by the middle of a game week, the RVs start to roll into town.

It is a beautiful college town with rolling hills. Mt. Nittany overlooks the stadium. The students tend to arrive early and make lots of noise. Being there for a "White Out" is really a happening. With more than 100,000 fans sporting white shirts and strong vocal cords, Penn State enjoys a very nice home-field advantage.

Barry Alvarez always believed the folks at Penn State treated the visiting team with nothing but class. You might think that is just a Pennsylvania native talking, but trust me, if he had a problem with something there, he would have said so. This is a town that loves its college football and everything that goes with a game day.

For a taste of the town, there are plenty of options. One year a group of us visited a joint called The Phyrst. What a trip. The place was up for grabs. It is an establishment with picnic tables, beer, wall-to-wall people, more beer, and a band called The Phyrst Family that plays an iPod full of sing-a-long tunes.

It is also one of those places where one table full of people will challenge another to gulp down a pitcher of beer, so if that isn't your idea of fun, maybe you should try another spot. I have to admit, the night we were there was a blast, and we lived to tell about it.

2. Ohio Stadium—Ohio State University. My allegiance to Buckeyes football left the building many years ago, as mentioned earlier, but I do enjoy watching Script Ohio. I am a sucker for tradition. I believe that is a big hook for college football, and watching that band routine is one of the best traditions in the game.

Much like Penn State fans, those in Ohio take their football very seriously. BTN analyst Gerry DiNardo has said Ohio State is the closest thing the Big Ten has to an SEC program. That can mean many things, but I believe part of what he is talking about is the enthusiasm fans have for their Buckeyes. Sometimes it is a tad is over the top, but it is very real.

When I went to school there, I was stunned by how closely the media outlets in Columbus covered that team. It might be in the middle of the World Series, but the *Columbus Dispatch* would have a much bigger story about some OSU player in the middle of the week than anything regarding the Fall Classic.

It is a simple case of feeding the beast, and a game day at the Horseshoe tends to be a pretty good show. Adding to the atmosphere these days is the fact that Wisconsin and Ohio State have developed a strong rivalry, which only makes the crowds a bit more feisty. A Badgers fan once asked me for advice about attending a game down there. "Wear a hard hat," was my response.

Among the spots you might want to hit, if there is room, is the Varsity Club, which has been around forever. It is very close to the stadium, and for Badgers fans I would compare it in some ways to the Big Ten Pub near Camp Randall Stadium. You will see a ton of diehard fans, and on a game day it is a sea of humanity. You might be better off going there the night before the game.

3. Kinnick Stadium—University of Iowa. As loud as it was in Camp Randall for the 2010 game with Ohio State, there are those who swear it was louder the following week in Iowa City when the Badgers played the Hawkeyes. The game was terrific, a back-and-forth affair with Wisconsin scoring in the final minute to win. Of course, when the clock struck zero, it became pretty quiet except for the Wisconsin fans going nuts.

Every Big Ten stadium has been renovated, except Minnesota, which built a new facility a few years ago. They did very nice work at Kinnick, making improvements while keeping the old-school look. Like many schools including Wisconsin, the Hawkeyes game management folks do a good job putting together a video board entrance for the home team, complete with AC/DC's classic song, "Back in Black."

Like Nebraska, there are no major professional sports franchises in the state, so Iowa football is huge. With all due respect to Iowa State, which has given the Hawks fits on the field, the University of Iowa is the big show. It might not have a 100,000-seat stadium, but it can sound as though there are at least that many fans in the stands for a big home game.

For some local flavor, try the Wig & Pen. Along the same lines as the Varsity Club, it is a great spot for sports fans who want a good sandwich or a pizza to go along with a cold beverage of your choice.

4. Michigan Stadium—University of Michigan. This place has moved up a few notches in my book, in large part because they did such a great job of renovating the press box, especially our broadcast booth. Yes, I am being selfish, so sue me.

For a long time, Wolverines fans have had the reputation of being quiet, kind of a wine-and-cheese crowd. That has changed maybe in part because they went through a stretch where winning ten games a season was no longer automatic. You could say the folks at Michigan loved tradition to a fault because before the 2011 season, the Wolverines had never hosted a night game. That finally changed last September when Michigan and Notre Dame played under the lights. It was an amazing game with the lead changing hands three times in the final two minutes. There was nothing "wine and cheese" about the crowd that night.

The last time the Badgers played in the Big House was 2010. Wisconsin overpowered Michigan, but for a brief time in the third quarter, the Wolverines were getting a little momentum. In a year when the Wolverines were not very good and the defense was terrible, the crowd was trying its best to help the home team. I had to admit, I was impressed.

Speaking of being impressed, I have always enjoyed a trip to Fraser's the night before a game. It has been a few years, but when in Ann Arbor for a football game, you should go. I keep recommending very casual pubs, and Frasers is very much a casual place with plenty of good burgers and cold beer. Back in the day there always seemed to be good-looking bartenders, as well, which never hurts. My guess is the tradition continues.

5. Spartan Stadium—Michigan State University. Because of the terrific radio booth and spacious media area, this is another of my professional favorites. Unlike their counterparts to the east, you cannot accuse MSU fans of being wine and cheese. Call it having a chip on their shoulder or whatever, but these fans can get pretty rowdy, and I say that as a compliment.

The campus also is very pretty, and I think it tends to be underrated in that regard. For sheer atmosphere, I think the basketball crowds are better, but perhaps all those Final Four appearances might have something to do with that.

I always thought it would be fun to be in Spartan Stadium for a Michigan State–Michigan game. For years and years many folks, including former Michigan running back Mike Hart, considered MSU to be the little brother, but since Mark Dantonio arrived in East Lansing, that has changed.

Downtown Lansing has a number of good entertainment options. My personal favorite is The Knight Cap, an old-school steak joint. While not necessarily a coat-and-tie establishment, it offers a little finer dining than my previous suggestions. It is a restaurant with a simple motto, which you can read on its coffee cups—"If you want home cooking, eat at home." If you enjoy a good old American steak dinner, give it a try.

Now, in no particular order, here are the rest of the Big Ten stops:

TCF Bank Stadium—University of Minnesota. A beautiful new on-campus stadium, something the Gophers have dearly needed for a long time. Probably best known for its enormous home locker room, TCF Bank Stadium should be the pride and joy of outgoing Athletics Director Joel Maturi, the former UW administrator who is one of the really good people I have met in sports.

With the land that was available to build the stadium, TCF is different from most because the field runs east-west and not north-south. From the press box, we can look to our left and get a nice view of the Minneapolis skyline. Badgers fans are in no hurry to see the Gophers get their program turned in the right direction, but that stadium should help the Gophers' efforts in moving up in the standings.

In a bigger city like Minneapolis, there are hundreds of dining options. Returning to the casual theme, I would suggest heading back downtown to the Loon Café. It is right down the street from Target Center and Target Field. On a weekend night, the people-watching can be pretty good. In fact, one evening on a basketball trip we discovered the Chicago Bulls were also in town. This was during the heyday of Michael Jordan and company. A group of us headed to the Loon for a few pops, and all of a sudden there was a commotion. We turned to look upstairs, and there was Jordan himself, cigar in hand and a big smile on his face. Seems he was celebrating his birthday, and he and his friends had reserved the upper level of the bar. Patrons who might otherwise have gone bar hopping hung around, either hoping to shake his hand, get an autograph, or maybe they were just waiting for him to buy a round for the house.

I think the Loon did a pretty good business that night.

Memorial Stadium—University of Illinois. There is plenty of space surrounding this old stadium, which makes it great for tailgating. Take a lap around the Illini's home field, and you will see what I am talking about. The grills are going, the kegs have been tapped, and the music is blaring. It is a quality scene for a program that has had its ups and downs.

While perhaps not as nationally recognized as Ohio or Michigan Stadium, the pillars on the outside of Memorial Stadium give the place a classic look. Since it sits in the flatlands of central Illinois, the wind can be nasty there. Keep that in mind if your visit to Champaign occurs later in the season.

I am sure there are some fine restaurants on the city's main drag, but as far as I am concerned, Houlihan's works just fine. Why Houlihan's? There happens to be one connected to perhaps the best hotel we visit on the circuit. Yes, I said the best hotel. It is called the I Hotel, and it is located a stone's throw from Memorial Stadium and Assembly Hall. When we arrive in Champaign, our crew rarely ventures far from the hotel. That means two things—we are boring, and the hotel is so nice, there is little reason to leave.

Ross Ade Stadium—Purdue University. Another excellent working environment. Truth be told, most of the booths in the Big Ten are very good, from the working space to the sight lines. I know the same cannot be said for NFL radio crews, who often work from a booth overlooking the 10-yard line, or even a corner of the end zone.

But enough about us. Perhaps some cynics might tell you that there is little that qualifies as special about the Boilermakers home field, but when Joe Tiller had things going in West Lafayette, that was a tough place to play. The fans can get very loud. Of course, the Purdue band features the World's Largest Drum, which is something any first-time visitor should make a point to see. Then again, since it is a really big drum, you can't really miss it.

The tough part for me about a trip to Purdue is we usually stay either out in the boonies or on a main drag just off I-65 with nothing but chain restaurants. I am okay with chains, but I am trying to give you more traditional hot spots.

For this Big Ten location, folks tell me you should head to Bruno's Swiss Inn. It gets high marks for its pizza and lasagna. Who doesn't like pizza and lasagna? I say go for it.

Ryan Field—Northwestern University. More than a decade ago, they dressed up the home of the Wildcats, and it is now a nice-looking facility. It just is not very big, and in a sense it lacks the intimacy of many other venues.

Make no mistake—Ryan Field has been a House of Horrors for the Badgers, who have not won in Evanston since 1999. Even though there usually are more Wisconsin fans than Northwestern backers for a game down there, too many times fans have driven back across the border in a lousy mood. In a pro sports town such as Chicago, the Wildcats struggle for attention. That is a shame because Pat Fitzgerald has done an excellent job with the program. I think it is safe to say that no team really likes going there. The atmosphere might be lacking, but the home team is pretty good.

When you go, check out Mustard's Last Stand, located on the west edge of the Ryan Field parking lot. It is what you think it is—a good spot to get yourself a pre- or postgame hot dog. The creative name of the place is reason enough to give it a try, right?

Memorial Stadium—Indiana University. This is another stadium with lots of space around it. They did an outstanding job of improving this football building in basketball-mad Bloomington. Similar to Assembly Hall, home of the hoops team, the stands along the sidelines reach to the sky. The bad news for IU is that usually you can have an entire row, and sometimes and entire section, to yourself.

They are doing what they can to attract fans of all ages to see a game. Behind the south end zone is a mini-football field where kids can run around and blow off some steam. Indiana football has struggled badly, but they are hoping Kevin Wilson can eventually turn things around. To be fair, the school has had terrible luck. A few years ago the Hoosiers seemed to have the perfect fit in Coach Terry Hoeppner, a man whose enthusiasm was hard not to appreciate. Sadly, he died before he really had a chance to get the program going. Since Hoeppner's tragic passing, the Hoosiers have been try-ing to get back on track.

Bloomington is another picturesque college town. A favorite dinner option for me has been Janko's Little Zagreb. There is noth-ing fancy here. You will see checkered tablecloths, and your adult beverage options are beer and wine, but oh my goodness, the food is good! You barely need a knife to cut your steak. It can get a little loud in there, but who cares? The folks are friendly, and you can look at any number of photos on the walls and get a good feel for the history of IU athletics.

As I get older, I find myself enjoying these trips a little more than I did in my younger days. I appreciate the enthusiasm fans have for their teams all across Big Ten country. Sure, some fan bases are more rabid than others, but every program has its loyal followers, and every town is worth a visit. I did not always feel that way. I will admit there was a time when a trip to Lafayette or Champaign did not thrill me. Maybe it is the improved working conditions. Or maybe it is the fact that most Big Ten cities have at least a couple of pretty good hotels.

At the risk of sounding like Big Ten commissioner Jim Delany's spokesman, I would not discourage you from going to any campus in this conference. Maybe there is no other Camp Randall Stadium, but I believe you would enjoy a trip anywhere in the league.

I know I can't wait to visit Lincoln, Nebraska, this fall. Now if anyone can recommend a place for a burger, I am all ears.

19

Basketball Venues

FOR MANY YEARS, a Badger road game meant bad news. As the program has grown, those memories are fading away. Of course, younger Wisconsin fans might not have any idea what I am talking about.

The fact is when a Bo Ryan–led team goes into an opposing arena, there usually is a pretty good atmosphere. That is because those fans understand that beating Wisconsin is hardly an easy task. The Badgers have spoiled enough parties in other cities to make opposing supporters aware that a visit from the Cardinal and White no longer means an automatic victory.

As Wisconsin has grown into a consistent contender in the Big Ten race, rivalries have developed, and in some cases picked up some steam, making for some big-time enthusiasm on cold winter nights.

With that in mind, here are my Top 5 opposing gyms, with the rest in no particular order. Again, I leave Nebraska out of the mix, as one visit over the semester break is hardly a fair sample size on which to judge a fan base.

1. Breslin Center—Michigan State University. I give a slight edge to the Spartans' home court, edging the No. 2 selection. The arena is intimate, and the student section, known as the Izzone, is top notch. The student section wraps around the court, which in the world of higher-end donor seating is something not every school chooses to do. Clad in their white shirts with green trim, fans in the Izzone look the part and make a ton of noise.

To me, an underrated part of MSU's game presentation is when they play the "Curly Shuffle" on the sound system during one of the timeouts. You have to respect anyone who pays tribute to the Three Stooges.

While the home team usually wins, the Badgers have sent the Izzone out of the arena broken-hearted on more than one occasion. Perhaps the most famous of the Badgers non–Big Ten title-clinching victories occurred in East Lansing. In a nutshell, the Breslin Center crowds are loud, they are organized, and they must be worth at least a couple of buckets to the home team for every game.

In a terrific game, the Badgers ruined the evening for Sparty and company, as they beat Michigan State in overtime 68–64. For Wisconsin, it was a banner night of a different sort.

2. Assembly Hall—University of Illinois. This is a very close second. The Orange Krush is another excellent student section. Through the years, that group has raised money for local charities, and like the Izzone, the students surround a good portion of the floor. The building is getting up there in years, but the Orange Krush helps keep the atmosphere fresh.

For years, part of the halftime show included the students forming a ring around the floor while Chief Illiniwek performed a dance. Native American nicknames have been a source of controversy, and the Chief's dance was the subject of much debate for several years. By the end of the 2007 season, U of I officials opted to remove the dance as part of the halftime festivities.

Another thing they used to do, and I don't think it was very controversial, was an old Blues Brothers bit, complete with two dudes decked out in the outfits that John Belushi and Dan Aykroyd made famous in the 1980 movie. During a timeout in the second half, the band would get cranked up, and the young men, wearing black suits, white shirts, black ties, and of course, sunglasses, would run out onto the floor and get the crowd going. I miss that.

3. Mackey Arena—Purdue University. With just two wins since the Nixon administration, this place has been a trip of nightmares for Wisconsin. It has been renovated, but there is little that is fancy about this arena, with bleacher seating throughout most of the facility. Like many older buildings, Mackey Arena can hold noise, and the Paint Crew, which is the name of the student section, makes plenty of noise.

What used to be odd about Mackey was that for years fans were prohibited from bringing their concession items to their seats. In other words, when someone bought a hot dog and a soft drink, he had to consume it in the concourse. For the media, they kept a water jug and a stack of paper cups at the end of our row. Eventually, some folks figured out that maybe it would be a good idea to allow fans to bring their food and drink to their seats.

I always felt badly for fans who sat behind us at Mackey. Our seats were actually slightly below court level, and there were several rows of bleacher seats directly behind us. So those poor folks probably had a better view of the back of our heads than they did the court itself. With the renovation, our position is court level, right by the visiting bench. Those behind us still might not have the best view, but it is a marked improvement.

Mackey Arena is a good facility, and I really appreciate the creativity of the student section names. When Gene Keady was on the bench, it was called the Gene Pool. The Paint Crew is not bad, either.

4. Assembly Hall—Indiana University. In basketball-crazy Indiana when the Hoosiers get it going, fans there are capable of blowing the roof off of that place. Coach Tom Crean inherited an awful situation following the departure of Kelvin Sampson, but there is much to sell at IU. When the home team is playing well, it is an extremely loud house.

Much like Indiana's football stadium, Assembly Hall has sideline seats that go halfway to the moon. The pitch is rather dramatic, as well. Put it this way—if you are uncomfortable with heights, I would not advise climbing to the top row. You might notice the world starting to spin a little bit.

The building is full of history. I remember when Brian Butch played at Wisconsin. He enjoys college basketball history, and he was eager to play in the building that Bob Knight helped make famous. It was extra special in 2008 when Butch banked in a three-point shot to give the Badgers a 68–66 victory against the 13th-ranked Hoosiers.

Behind one of the baskets, the Indiana NCAA Championship banners are hanging. For years, people would swear that when the visiting team was shooting at that basket, the banners would sway. All part of home-court advantage, right?

5. Williams Arena—University of Minnesota. I have to include The Barn in my Top 5. Speaking of a nothing-fancy facility—this arena certainly fits that description. On a night when it is 20 below zero, it can feel like it is 90 degrees or more in the upper level of this joint.

With an elevated floor, Bo Ryan has a little tradition when his team practices there the night before a game. It is a drop of about 3', and no doubt some players have been fearful of getting hurt. Bo has a little drill where he has his players, especially the freshmen, go after a loose ball and slide off the floor just so they know they can fall off the edge but still live to tell about it.

Williams Arena reminds me of the UW Field House in that it is an old, loud building with fans who are there not to be seen but rather to see their team in action. One thing is for certain, the atmosphere is very good when the Badgers are in town.

As for the rest, here they are in no particular order:

Value City Arena—Ohio State University. I miss St. John Arena. When Gary Williams was OSU's coach, he pushed to have the students close to the floor. After he left for Maryland, Randy Ayers put together some excellent teams in the early 1990s with stars such as Jim Jackson. Old St. John Arena would rock.

Value City Arena reminds me of a scaled-down United Center, home of the Chicago Bulls and Blackhawks. It is not a bad place, but like many newer arenas, much of the intimacy is lost. In the last couple of years, school officials have moved the students so they surround much of the floor. That made for a crazy-loud atmosphere right behind our broadcast location during the 2011 season. In February of that year, the Badgers gave Ohio State its first loss of the season, which also completed the rare feat of beating the No. 1 team in the nation in both football and hoops during the same sports season.

To say the least, OSU fans were more than ready for the March rematch. Prior to tip-off, one of the nicer comments from the student body was, "Hey Jordan Taylor, you suck!" Our location was right by the Wisconsin bench, with students about 3" behind us. Before the game, one of the students looked at us and said, "We have no problem with you guys—it's about them!" as he pointed to the Badger players going through their warm-ups.

As tip-off drew closer, the students backed off with the R-rated language, but they were vocal all day long. In what had often been a bland venue, Value City Arena came alive, confirming that the Badgers had become a strong rival.

Carver Hawkeye Arena—University of Iowa. When Dr. Tom Davis had the Hawkeyes rolling, sellout crowds were the norm, and in a state without a major professional sports franchise, Iowa basketball was a very big deal. Every call that went against the home team was a lousy call, and the loyal Iowa fans would let the officials know what they were thinking.

I do enjoy Iowa fans. Before a game, they can kill you with kindness. When the game begins, you believe they just want to kill you.

When you walk into the arena, you are in the top row of the seats. There is no mid-level entrance into the bowl, which can make it difficult for those who would rather not negotiate all those steps to get from Row 35 to Row 5.

Otherwise, if Iowa gets its basketball program cranked up again, there is no doubt the Hawks will regain a big home-court advantage.

Welsh-Ryan Arena—Northwestern University. The smallest of the Big Ten arenas usually has a huge turnout of Badgers fans. It probably could use a face-lift, but I enjoy it because it is the "anti-oversized" building. With all those Wisconsin fans in the house, there is plenty of noise in Welsh-Ryan, proving that a bigger arena is not always better.

And let's face it—through the years the Wildcats have given the Badgers lots of trouble in Evanston. The student section is rather small, but it can be pretty good. Even Bo Ryan likes the shirts they have been wearing the last couple of years. It is pretty simple stuff—the shirts say "Make Shots." Given Coach Bill Carmody's system that relies quite a bit on perimeter shooting, "Make Shots" makes sense.

Bryce Jordan Center—Penn State University. Truth be told, this building probably is too big for basketball, but in Central Pennsylvania, they wanted a facility large enough to hold concerts and other such events.

For some games, they just close off part of the arena's upper level. A notable exception occurred when the Badgers played there in 2009. The Philadelphia Phillies were a few months removed from winning the World Series, and the day the Badgers visited State College, the championship trophy was on display at the BJC. That alone drew quite a crowd as well as the interest of lifelong Phillies fans Bo Ryan and assistant coach Gary Close.

Normally, Bo has a pregame routine that includes our radio interview followed by a quick chat with the TV folks. He then retreats to the coach's locker room, but that day he made an exception. Bo, his son, Matt, as well as Gary just had to have a photo with the World Series trophy.

Damn Phillies.

The Nittany Lions' old hoops home was Rec Hall, a boisterous gym that would seat about 8,000. Talk about intimate. The students were right on top of the floor. I mean right on top. When a player was inbounding the ball from the sideline, he generally had a student breathing down his neck.

The Badgers were Penn State's final opponent at Rec Hall. Other than the fact Wisconsin lost, the most vivid memory I have of that day was flying out of State College during a huge snow storm. At that time, the UW used a charter service out of Alaska, so I guess a 14" snow fall was no big deal. I know a few of us were looking out the window of the plane just to see how much snow was gathering on the wings.

Such is the glamorous life of Big Ten travel.

Crisler Center—University of Michigan. Another building that has been renovated, and this one *really* needed it. A few years ago the home locker room was upgraded, but most of the building looked untouched for years.

While there certainly is basketball tradition at Michigan, there is no mistaking the image that this is a football school. However, the student section is pretty good, and since it is seated behind the scorer's table as well as the team benches, it shows up well on television. With the program improving and the facility upgraded, there are strong signs that Michigan basketball is on its way back.

In 2011, the Badgers beat the Wolverines when Josh Gasser banked home a three-point shot at the horn. As you might imagine,

Michigan fans were disappointed and angry. As a few were leaving their seats, they looked at us and started shaking their heads. When we were in a commercial break, I just told them we were pulling for them in their next game, which happened to be against Michigan State.

It's all about knowing your audience.

Generally speaking, the Big Ten arenas are pretty good. Some are great. The more sedate crowds tend to make some noise when the Badgers come to town. The Badgers no longer play the role of the Washington Generals going up against the Globetrotters. If Penn State beats Wisconsin in front of a half-empty Bryce Jordan Center, it is a big deal for the fans who did show up. Maybe that is a back-handed compliment, but it is a tribute to the rise of Badger basketball.

20

Top 10 Football Moments

SINCE MY FOOTBALL PLAY-BY-PLAY DUTIES only go back to the 1994 season, there will be a couple of omissions that might seem strange, such as when the Badgers clinched a Rose Bowl bid on the other side of the world in 1993. Then there was Darrell Bevell's dramatic fourth-quarter touchdown run in the Rose Bowl and the moment when UCLA quarterback Wayne Cook was tackled and time ran out in Pasadena, giving Wisconsin its first Rose Bowl victory.

Even by leaving out those highlights, there are some tough cuts in the Top 10 moments from 1994–2011. Among the honorable-mention plays:

- Nick Davis' punt return for a touchdown in the 1998 Big Ten title-clinching game against Penn State.
- Jamar Fletcher's 1998 and 1999 interception returns for touchdowns against Drew Brees and the Purdue Boilermakers.
- Tyler Donovan's amazing touchdown pass to Travis Beckum at Ohio State in 2007. Donovan avoided a strong Buckeyes rush, scrambled, and found Beckum, who made a big sliding catch for the score.
- Tarek Saleh's game-sealing sack at Michigan in 1994. Coming off a Rose Bowl season, the Badgers had high hopes for another big year in 1994. However, a tie with Purdue followed by a stunning loss to Minnesota and suddenly there was talk of going

from Rose Bowl to no bowl. To say the least, not many expected the Badgers to win at Michigan, but win they did. Bevell hooked up with "Touchdown" Tony Simmons for a pair of scores, but Wisconsin fans were still worried about a Wolverines rally. Saleh's sack of Todd Collins closed the door to that possibility.

Now for my Top 10:

10. Matt Davenport's field goal at Northwestern. The previous week the Badgers needed a field goal in the closing seconds to beat Indiana in Madison. Elated with what occurred, long snapper Mike Schneck jumped on his kicker, resulting in Schneck dislocating his elbow. One week later the Badgers were in another nail-biter, this time with Northwestern. A year earlier Northwestern stole a win when it scored late following a Ron Dayne fumble. In 1997, it was the Wildcats' turn to suffer. Leading late and driving to what might have been a clinching touchdown, Northwestern fumbled. Quarterback Mike Samuel helped move the Badgers to the NU 30. There were a few pieces to this drama. First, it was a 48-yard field goal try—not the longest ever, but certainly no chip shot. Second, it was a night game, and the grass was getting very wet with the evening dew, which could make the footing tricky and the football a little heavier. Third, there was a new long snapper. Mike Solwold turned out to be very good, but that was his first game in that role. The snap was not very pretty, but it was good enough, and Davenport did the rest.

"He did it again! Matt Davenport did it again!" was the call as Money nailed the kick with six seconds to play, giving the Badgers a huge victory and a little payback for the 1996 heartbreaker.

9. Nortman's fake punt at Iowa. Before he coached his first game at Wisconsin, Bret Bielema said, "I always want to be the aggressor." He sure was aggressive in Iowa City in 2010. It was a seesaw game, and in the fourth quarter the Badgers were lining up to punt on fourth-and-4 in their own territory. Brad Nortman took the snap, and as Iowa peeled back to set up a return, the Wisconsin punter took off. The Hawkeyes were totally caught off guard, and Nortman ran 17 yards for a critical first down, allowing the Badgers to continue their drive, capped by Montee Ball's touchdown run with 1:06 to play.

An honorable-mention moment from that game came from linebacker Mike Taylor. In Iowa's final possession, the Hawkeyes were getting close to field-goal range, but they also were out of timeouts. Iowa tried a short pass to running back Adam Robinson, and Taylor tackled him inbounds. The Hawks were unable to line up and spike the ball, and the Badgers left town with a 31–30 victory and the Heartland Trophy, a fairly new but prized possession in this rivalry.

8. Stocco's quarterback draw vs. Michigan. After the Badgers beat Michigan in 1994, they lost the next six meetings. Every game but one was very competitive, but the Wolverines always found a way to win.

In 2005, Barry Alvarez finally got the best of a Lloyd Carr–coached team. It was the Big Ten season opener under the lights at Camp Randall. Late in the game, Michigan led 20–16, but the Badgers were driving. Quarterback John Stocco and tailback Brian Calhoun were doing much of the heavy-lifting that night, and in the final half-minute Wisconsin had a third-and-goal at the Michigan 4-yard line.

As the story goes, receiver's coach Henry Mason suggested a quarterback draw could work. Stocco was a much better athlete than advertised, and the Badgers thought the Wolverines would not be expecting such a play. It worked to perfection as Stocco scored with 24 seconds remaining, giving the Badgers a 23–20 victory. It was quite a way to start Alvarez's final Big Ten season.

7. Schabert to Evans vs. Ohio State. You could argue that this moment should be higher on the list. The Buckeyes came to town as the defending national champions and riding a 19-game winning streak. Along the way OSU won several close games. During the run to the BCS title in 2002, half of OSU's victories were one-score games, including a 19–14 win against the Badgers in Madison.

In 2003, the teams met again in Camp Randall Stadium. It was a wild night. Earlier in the day it was warm and humid. Then the rain arrived. In the first half, it was a downpour. By the end of the game, the temperature took a nosedive, and summer was long gone. The game was a slugfest. Tied at 10 with five-and-a-half minutes to play, it appeared the Buckeyes were building momentum. They had just scored, and Wisconsin was facing a second-and-9 from its own 21. Earlier in the game, OSU linebacker Robert Reynolds had put quarterback Jim Sorgi in a choke hold, forcing Sorgi to the sidelines. Enter backup Matt Schabert for a moment that most of us can only dream about.

For more than three quarters, Ohio State had shutout star receiver Lee Evans. That changed on one very big play. The Badgers called it "56 Jerk." The play called for Evans to run an out-and-up against cornerback Chris Gamble. It was a blow-by. Evans broke open, and Schabert hit him in stride for one of the more electrifying touchdowns in stadium history.

6. Sparky's fumble return at Purdue. In 2004, the Badgers were Purdue's Homecoming opponent. The previous week the Badgers had won at Ohio State. I will never forget talking to Alvarez the week before those two games. He honestly believed he had a better team than the Buckeyes. He was right, and the Badgers proved it by pounding Ohio State in Columbus. He also knew Purdue was better than Ohio State that year. Wisconsin went into the game ranked No. 10 Purdue was No. 5, and Kyle Orton's name was being thrown around as a legitimate Heisman Trophy contender.

Clearly, the Badgers' calling card that season was their defense. In 1951, Wisconsin had a lights-out good defense that allowed just 5.9 points per game called the Hard Rocks. In 2004, Mike Lucas dubbed the group the Hard Knocks. For most of the season, it was simply dominant, led by defensive end Erasmus "Ras" James. Wisconsin held its first five opponents to seven points or less. When I prepared for each week's broadcast, I made a point to find out who the team's *third*-string quarterback might be, just in case the other two were knocked out of the game.

At Purdue, it was James who was injured. He was on the receiving end of a low block from Boilermakers tight end Charles Davis. Ras never seemed to be the same the rest of the season. In West Lafayette that day, the UW defense was doing a great job on Orton and the Purdue offense, but the Wisconsin offense was struggling.

Trailing 17–7 in the fourth quarter, the Badgers drew closer on a John Stocco touchdown pass to tailback Booker Stanley. Still, Purdue was in position to run out the clock, and it appeared the Boilermakers would do just that. On third-and-short, Orton found room as he ran a bootleg. He had picked up the first down, but suddenly defensive back Robert Brooks came in and chopped the quarterback, sending him airborne as the ball popped out. Cornerback Scott Starks scooped up the loose ball and returned it 40 yards for a touchdown.

My radio description was as follows:

"Here's the boot, to the right. Orton on the run—has the first down—as he gets helicoptered! Ball is loose! Badgers have it! Here comes Starks! At the 20. At the 10. At the 5. Touchdown Wisconsin!" I really let it rip on that call as it was the most stunning moment I have witnessed. I mean the game was over, and it all turned on that play.

Purdue did have time to drive down the field in the closing moments, but the Boilers' Ben Jones missed a 42-yard field goal try, allowing Wisconsin to win the game 20–17.

For quite a while, Bret Bielema and I had some fun with how I called Starks' touchdown. It was a bang-bang play that required the officials to look at a replay to make sure Orton was not down before he fumbled. I figured right away that there would be a review, so I said on the air, "Badgers have the lead—at least for the moment."

Bret ragged on me, thinking I did not have faith in his defense (he was in his first year as defensive coordinator). That was not my thought at the time, but later I just rolled with it. "Yeah Bret, I had all the faith in the world that Purdue would drive the ball on your defense, and its kicker would then miss a field goal!" It is always easier to laugh after a big win, right?

5. Casillas punt block at Minnesota. The 2004 Purdue game was the game that surprised me the most, but the 2005 Battle for the Axe at the Metrodome is a close second. Minnesota running back Laurence Maroney was terrific, rushing for 258 yards. Fellow back Gary Russell added 139 yards of his own, and his touchdown gave the Gophers a 34–24 lead with three-and-a-half minutes to play.

The Badgers fought back as Stocco hooked up with Brandon Williams for a score, pulling the Badgers within three with 2:10 remaining. Wisconsin needed to get a three-and-out, and the odds of that happening seemed remote. Yet the Badgers were able to stop the Gophers, forcing a punt. Punter Justin Kucek mishandled the snap, and after he regained control of the ball he tried to roll off to his right, rugby-style, to get the punt away. Wisconsin's Jonathan Casillas, who had come close to blocking a few punts earlier in the season, was able to get this one. The ball rolled into the end zone for what seemed like forever before Ben Strickland pounced on it, giving Wisconsin a 38–34 shocker.

"The snap is clean—oh, he muffed it. Now he tries to roll off—the kick is blocked! It's loose in the end zone! It's still loose! The Badgers cover it up! Touchdown, Wisconsin! There it is! Ben Strickland comes out of there! The Badgers block the punt, and they take the lead with 30 seconds left at the Metrodome!"

I really like Minnesota's new TCF Bank Stadium, but I kind of miss those games at the Metrodome. The building is a little dumpy, but I enjoyed broadcasting games there, in large part because the games always were so entertaining. We also had a great view of the fans below us. It was a total shock. I rate this game slightly ahead of Purdue in terms of great moments simply because of the rivalry. In recent years, I believe it is safe to say that Gophers fans have developed a genuine dislike for all things Wisconsin Badgers. That October afternoon in 2005 only added more fuel to the fire.

4. Hail Russell to Jeff. It may be the most important pass play in Wisconsin history that did not result in a touchdown. Officially, it was fourth-and-6 at the Michigan State 43-yard line. The Spartans were leading the 2011 Big Ten Championship game 39–34. The play might very well have been the Badgers last chance to win the game. Wilson was flushed from the pocket and moved off to his left. For an instant, he thought about running for the first down, but MSU had him covered. Wilson then looked deep to the right side and let it fly. Waiting for the ball, along with two Spartan defenders, was Jeff Duckworth. The sophomore receiver went into attack mode, leaping into the air and pulling down the pass at the Michigan State 7-yard line. One play later, Montee Ball zipped into the end zone to score what proved to be the title-clinching touchdown.

3. Wendell Bryant sacks Cade McNown. It seems Rose Bowl games are always pretty exciting. That certainly has been the case for the Badgers. The 1999 game was especially entertaining. Ron Dayne ran for 246 yards and four touchdowns. UCLA had plenty of weapons on offense, and the game turned into a bit of a shootout featuring the Bruins passing attack vs. the Badgers running game. Naturally, such a contest came down to a big defensive play. Actually, Jamar Fletcher turned in a huge play earlier in the fourth quarter when he picked off a Cade McNown pass and ran it back for a touchdown.

Leading 38–31 late in the game, the Badgers were forced to punt, giving McNown one more chance to force overtime. On fourth-and-10 from the UCLA 46, Wendell Bryant sacked the Bruins quarterback, giving the underdog Badgers their second Rose Bowl triumph.

2. David Gilreath kickoff return vs. Ohio State. The buildup to the 2010 Wisconsin–Ohio State game was unreal. It seemed every branch of the ESPN empire was in Madison—ESPN, ESPN HD, ESPN Radio, and ESPN Game Day. There were trucks and cables everywhere. The weather was perfect, and for the first time in 13 years, the No. 1 team in America was in town. I just hoped the game would live up the hype. If you are a Badgers fan, you know that it most certainly did.

Gilreath has the UW career record for kickoff return yards, leading the field by 676 yards. It was a 97-yard effort that Badgers fans will always remember. A superbly blocked return, Gilreath raced untouched to the house. The final blow came from Bradie Ewing, who engulfed the kicker, something Ewing is quick to point out. At some point after the game, I congratulated him on delivering such a block. "Thanks, but it was the kicker." Those guys just never get any respect.

"Touchdown Wisconsin! And this game is underway with —a—bang!"

There are those who say that Gilreath's return set off the loudest roar anyone can remember at Camp Randall.

Wisconsin dominated the first half, but Ohio State made it a three-point game in the fourth quarter. The Badgers answered with a James White touchdown run followed by a Philip Welch field goal. And when Blake Sorensen intercepted a Terrelle Pryor pass late in the game, the party in Madison ramped up in a big way.

1. Ron Dayne breaks the record. The Gilreath return is close, and with all the media for the 2010 game, the hype was incredible, but for pure joy, I am not sure anything can beat Dayne's record run in 1999. As I mentioned earlier, the run featured everything that made Dayne a star. The day, and that moment in particular, seemed to be a confirmation that Wisconsin football was running with the big boys. The perfect weather, the tens of thousands of "Dayne 33" towels, and the team clinching another Big Ten title and a trip to the Rose Bowl puts this moment at the top of the list.

I am looking forward to future seasons to see whether there are some new candidates for my Top 10 list. With the way things have gone the last few years, it is almost certain there will be more moments worthy of consideration.

21

Top 10 Basketball Moments

IN THE PAST QUARTER CENTURY, the Wisconsin basketball team has had its share of dramatic moments, from buzzer-beaters to big defensive stops at the ends of games. It always helps when those moments are on a big stage, such as a spotlight regular season game against a highly ranked opponent or a matchup in the NCAA Tournament. However, sometimes the stage is not so big, but perhaps that is part of the beauty of trying to select ten specific games. As difficult as it is to leave off some of the football drama, it is even more of a challenge in basketball. Wisconsin basketball fans might recall many of these Top 10 moments as though they happened yesterday. Others might require a little more thought.

Having said that, here goes with my Top 10 Moments covering UW hoops:

10. Brian Good at the horn in Iowa City. For a time, Iowa had given the Badgers some major beatings. Some lowlights included a 105–65 trouncing in 1985 followed by a 101–48 thumping the following season. By the early 1990s, Wisconsin was getting a little payback. It wasn't winning by 50 points, but Wisconsin was finally getting a little streak going against the Hawkeyes. On February 16, 1991, the Badgers were trying to beat the Hawks for a fifth straight time. To put it mildly, the game was choppy and at times a little chippy. Words were exchanged, and the always-vocal Iowa fans were looking for some Badger blood. Down 55–53 in the final seconds, Badgers guard Brian Good drilled a three-pointer as time expired, giving Wisconsin a 56–55 stunner. It led to a less-than-stellar professional broadcast moment for yours truly. A UW employee was helping us with statistics that night, and as Good made the big shot, I gave my part-time stats man a high five, not exactly the most professional thing to do. Since we were able to leave Carver Hawkeye Arena alive, I could only guess that the fans were too shocked to notice.

9. Little Barkley beats the Gophers. In recent years, I have gotten to know former Minnesota standout Kevin Lynch. He tells the story of how he liked to play at the UW Field House and how one night he kept making eye contact with a Wisconsin cheerleader. For those who remember, I doubt that Lynch struggled very much finding a date, but why let a game get in the way of getting one more phone number?

Anyway, Lynch also remembers the January 22, 1990, matchup with the Badgers. That year's UW team had just four conference wins and went into the Minnesota game with a 1–4 league record. Even with a sub-.500 record, Lynch understood how tough the Badgers could be at home, especially with players such as Patrick Tompkins, a burly forward whom Lynch referred to as "Little Barkley," after NBA Hall of Famer Charles Barkley. This was a showcase game with ESPN and Dick Vitale in the house. After the Badgers had built a big lead, the No. 21 Gophers rallied. The game was tied at 75. With :01 remaining, the Badgers' Kurt Portmann was the trigger man on a baseline out-of-bounds play. Little Barkley flashed to the bucket and received a perfect lob for a lay-in at the horn. From our vantage point, I thought Tompkins tossed in a soft dunk, but all he really did was drop the ball through the basket. Fans rushed the court, and Dickie V gave his famous shout of "oooooohhhhh, ooooohh-hhhhh, oooohhhhh." In a season of few highlights, that was a very memorable night.

8. Jay Peters over Terrell Brandon. Oregon's old home for basketball was McArthur Court, which at one time was college basketball's second-oldest facility. It reminded many of the old Boston Garden. On November 24, 1990, the Badgers opened their season in Eugene. Earlier that day the football team ended its first season under Barry Alvarez with a tough 14–9 loss at Michigan State.

The basketball game was terrific and needed overtime to settle the issue. In the final seconds, the Badgers were down two and had to go the length of the floor. Jay Peters brought up the ball with Terrell Brandon checking him. This is the same Terrell Brandon who went on to become the eleventh overall pick in the 1991 NBA Draft, and among his professional stops was a two-year stint with the Milwaukee Bucks. As he brought the ball up court, Peters had to change direction a couple of times, but managed to get a decent look at the hoop, and he was able to stick a jumper at the horn. Jay has done very well in the business world. He sits in the courtside seats at the Kohl Center, and to this day when I introduce him to someone, I mention that shot at McArthur Court. I have to say I was not surprised to see Jay doing well in the real world. After his big shot, it was a happy group of players who were boarding the bus back to the team hotel. Jay was happy enough, but I could not help but notice that he was reading the *Wall Street Journal*.

7. Kam Taylor vs. Michigan State. In his Badgers career, Kammron Taylor hit a lot of big shots, including a buzzer-beater to beat UNC–Wilmington. On March 3, 2007, it was not quite a buzzer-beater, but it was close enough for me, and I am not sure I ever felt better for a player. The 2006–07 team made some history. It won 30 games and for one week was ranked No. 1 in the nation.

However, there would be no titles, and the NCAA Tournament run ended in the second round. The previous Sunday the Badgers played at Ohio State. A Wisconsin victory that day plus one more win against the Spartans would have given Bo Ryan's team the undisputed league title. Late in the first half, Brian Butch dislocated his elbow. The game was a grinder with the short-handed Badgers hanging in there in a matchup of No. 1 vs. No. 2. Leading 48–47, the Buckeyes fouled Taylor, putting the senior guard on the line for a mammoth one-and-one. Taylor missed the front end, and Ohio State rebounded. After Mike Conley's drive gave OSU the lead, the Badgers had one more chance, but Ron Lewis blocked Taylor's final attempt.

Six days later, the Badgers were in another close game against rival Michigan State. Less than two weeks earlier, the Spartans had beaten the top-ranked Badgers, setting off a huge celebration in East Lansing. It looked as though Tom Izzo's team would strike again as it led 50–49. A few moments earlier, Taylor had missed a jumper. With the clock ticking, Taylor launched a deep three and made it. After such a crushing loss a few days earlier, and after missing a big shot moments before in the rematch, it showed a lot that Ryan went back to Taylor for one more try. It also spoke volumes for Taylor that he delivered. It made for a great final home game of the season.

6. Brian Butch goes glass in Bloomington. In more ways than one, the night of February 13, 2008, marked the beginning of the end of the Kelvin Sampson era at Indiana. The Hoosiers had a very good team. With players such as Eric Gordon and D.J. White, there were many in college basketball who thought IU could be a very tough out in March. However, stories of potential NCAA violations were circulating, and by the time the Badgers arrived in Bloomington, those stories had become front-page news across the state.

Still, the game was big. The Badgers were coming off a close loss to Purdue and badly needed a road win to remain in the thick of the conference race. The back-and-forth game went down to the final second. Gordon's two free throws gave Indiana a 66–65 lead. The Badgers had one final possession. From left of the circle, Marcus Landry gave up the ball to Brian Butch, and with five seconds to play he fired up a rocket that banked hard off the glass and dropped through. Leading 68–66, the outcome remained in doubt. Indiana played on, and Jamarcus Ellis actually had a decent look at what would have been a game-winning shot, but the ball bounced off the rim, giving the Badgers a critical victory en route to a Big Ten title.

5. Pop's spin move vs. Florida State. It is amazing how Bo Ryan has raised the bar at Wisconsin. In the 2008–09 season, the Badgers managed *only* 20 victories. They finished fourth in the Big Ten. At one time that was really big stuff, but in Ryan's first decade as UW coach, fourth place represents a low point. It is quite the run when a team can finish fourth or better for such a long stretch. In 2009, Wisconsin was one of those bubble teams, but it made the NCAA Tournament as a No. 12 seed. Its first-round matchup would be against fifth-seeded Florida State in Boise, Idaho. The first half was ugly as the Badgers could not find the basket, but as often happens with Wisconsin, the second half was a different story. Keaton Nankivil started to heat up. Jason Bohannon hit a very cold-blooded three. Eventually the game went into overtime. Somewhat similar to Kam Taylor, Travon Hughes hit his share of pressure shots. Earlier that season, the player they called "Pop" drove into the lane for a bucket that beat Virginia Tech. Apparently happy to see another ACC opponent, Hughes struck again. Trailing 59–58 with about five seconds remaining, Hughes worked the left-lane line, then put on a little spin move into the key, absorbed contact, and with his strength still managed to score and draw a foul in the process. It finished a gutsy comeback for a gutsy team. As Bo will always say, go find another team that loses six straight conference games—as the Badgers did that season—and still earn a trip to the NCAA Tournament without winning its own league tourney.

4. Flowers for three, plus a steal. On December 29, 2007, the Badgers played Texas in Austin. During practice on the night of the 28th, Travon Hughes suffered a badly sprained ankle. I will admit it. I was afraid that without Hughes the Badgers might get drilled. On the contrary, it was one of the best road victories in UW history. In another close game, the ninth-rated Longhorns led 66–64. The Badgers had 11.3 seconds to go the length of the floor. Michael Flowers, moving to his right, rubbed off a Brian Butch screen near the top of the key. Butch popped to the left wing, and when the Texas defender went under the pick, Flowers had space to fire a three. He made it, but his best effort was yet to come. With 02.7 seconds to play, the Horns inbounded, but Flowers darted into the passing lane and stole the ball. His momentum was taking him out of bounds, so Flowers simply tossed the ball high into the air as time ran out. For a December game, it was very emotional. In his post-game interview on ESPN, even Ryan was a little choked up. That season the Badgers rolled to the Big Ten regular season and conference tournament championship, advancing to the Sweet 16 before bowing out to Stephen Curry and Davidson.

3. Owens for three vs. Tulsa. In the 2003 NCAA Tournament, the Badgers opened with an 81–74 victory against Weber State. The second-round opponent for fifth-seeded Wisconsin would be No. 13 seed Tulsa. With a little more than 3:30 remaining, the Badgers trailed 58–45. I thought it was over and said as much on the air. It was my mistake, and I was thrilled to be so wrong. The Badgers went on an 11–0 run. Then down 60–58 with :12 left, they had a shot to win it. Tulsa made the logical decision to surround Devin Harris and let somebody else beat it. Harris dribbled across the top of the circle and then started to drive. As the Tulsa defense converged, Harris found Freddie Owens open in the left corner. Freddie was another player who was known to hit pressure shots, and on March 22, 2003, he hit the biggest shot of his career, splashing a triple to give the Badgers a 61–60 victory and sending Wisconsin to the Sweet 16.

2. "The Badgers are dancing. The Badgers are dancing!" The 1997 season marked the final year before the Big Ten started its conference tournament. The Badgers went into the final regular season game with a 17–9 record, 10–7 in the league. It was very much a bubble team, or so thought the experts. No. 2 Minnesota came to town for the regular season finale. It already had clinched the conference title, but the conventional wisdom was that the Gophers still considered the game important to help secure a top seed in the NCAA Tournament. The Field House was electric. Down by one late in the game, guard Ty Calderwood was at the free throw line for two shots. He made them both to give the Badgers a 66–65 lead, but Minnesota had a final possession. Calderwood and Sam Okey combined to force a Gophers turnover as time expired, setting off a wild celebration in Madison. On the air I shouted, "The Badgers are dancing. The Badgers are dancing in 1997, and the Field House is up for grabs!" After the game, my wife, Linda, and I were out running some errands before meeting up with friends for dinner. After returning home, my mother called to ask if I am on the NCAA Tournament selection committee. I had no clue why she would ask such a question. Turns out some of the ESPN folks used the radio call of the final play and had some fun at my expense for making the assumption that the Badgers were going to make the field. When we met some friends at dinner, one of them told me that ESPN was killing me. So it goes. The next night I felt very good when the Badgers made the field as a No. 7 seed. Such a high seed made it pretty obvious that the Badgers were in good shape, win or lose against Minnesota. Take that, worldwide leader!

2a. *(Yeah, I am cheating.)* **Devin's free throw for the title.** In Bo Ryan's first year as Wisconsin's head coach, the Badgers won a piece of the conference title. In his second year, they were the outright champs, clinching the crown in a classic game against Illinois. It was March 5, 2003. The Illini had some terrific young talent such as Deron Williams, Dee Brown, and Luther Head. With two minutes to play, the Badgers led 59–52, but Illinois had one more push. A three from Brian Cook followed by a drive from Brown and then another jumper from Cook tied the game with 11 seconds to go. Working for the final shot, Devin Harris drove left of the lane, but the ball was knocked out of bounds as time ran out. For an instant, everyone in the Kohl Center thought the game was headed to overtime. However, Brown was called for a foul with four-tenths of a second remaining, sending Harris to the line for two shots. His first attempt went around the rim and out. To say the least, there was a little tension in the air. Harris gathered himself and calmly sank the second free throw, giving his team a one-point lead. Cook was unable to get off the final shot in time, and he missed it anyway as the Badgers won another Big Ten championship.

1. Badgers beat Purdue for Final Four Berth. There was no last second shot here, but how can I leave out such a moment? Do I really need to explain this one?

1a. *(I'm cheating again.)* **Wisconsin 71, Ohio State 67.** The last time the Badgers had beaten a No. 1 team was March 1962, and that team also happened to be the Buckeyes. It is tough to pick one moment from the February 12, 2011, classic with Ohio State, but anytime a team rallies from 15 points down in the second half to knock off the top-ranked team in the country, it needs to be on the list. The game looked pretty bleak right up until the home team ripped off 15 straight points to tie the game. Jordan Taylor was unreal, scoring 27 points, and Mike Bruesewitz hit a mammoth three in the final minute. All I could think to say was, "It's déjà vu in Madison!" In October, the football team beat the No. 1-ranked Buckeyes, and four months later the same story was unfolding at the Kohl Center. As the crowd rushed the floor, it was fun seeing football players Jay Valai and Nick Toon joining in the fun. There is nothing like beating the top-rated team, especially the way the Badgers were able to do it.

I have to say leaving the December 2009 Duke game off this list is a tough one, but I will put that on an honorable mention list. Again, it was not for a specific moment but for the night in general. The Badgers never trailed the No. 6 Blue Devils en route to a 73–69 victory. Of course, Duke went on to win the national championship, but on one night in early December, the Badgers were the toast of college basketball. The next morning Mike Lucas, Barry Alvarez, and I flew to Hawaii for that Saturday's football game, and when we arrived at our hotel and bumped into some players, the first thing they asked about was the basketball game.

Certainly there are other moments and games that are worthy, but I already have turned a 10-game list into 12. If I kept going, and believe me I could, the Top 10 would be a Top 20 or more. It is tough leaving off Jason Johnsen's game-winner at Michigan State in 1993, giving Stu Jackson his first road victory against a ranked opponent. It is another game worthy of at least honorable-mention status. Then there was the 1996 game at the Field House, when Sean Daugherty nailed a jumper at the horn to give the Badgers a 54–52 victory against Penn State. It was a critical game in Dick Bennett's first season, and that shot helped Wisconsin earn an NIT bid. That is the beauty of being around a program that has grown like Wisconsin. The trouble is not coming up with ten. The challenge is what to exclude.

That is a nice problem to have.

22

Back to the Top

THE 2008 FOOTBALL SEASON PROVIDED SOME HARSH LESSONS for the Badgers and Coach Bret Bielema. Keep in mind that for many Wisconsin sports fans, poor years are redefined, but the 7–6 record of 2008 was a downer.

After rolling through their three non-conference games, the Badgers began conference play at Michigan, a program rebuilding under first-year head coach Rich Rodriguez. It was a rare sight—a Wolverines team that was more than beatable at home. At halftime, the Badgers led 19–0. The Michigan Stadium crowd was booing the home team. Heading into the locker room, some UW players were yapping away at their stunned opponents.

It was a bad idea.

In the second half, everything that could have gone wrong did go wrong. The Wolverines scored 27 points in the second half to take an eight-point lead into the closing minutes. The Badgers rallied as Allan Evridge threw a touchdown pass to David Gilreath with 13 seconds to play. A successful two-point conversion would send the game to overtime, but Wisconsin was called for an illegal formation, wiping out the play. A second attempt to tie the game fell incomplete, and the Badgers began the Big Ten schedule with a shocking 27–25 loss in Ann Arbor.

The following week, the Badgers took another shot to the solar plexus. Leading Ohio State 17–13 in the fourth quarter, freshman quarterback Terrelle Pryor led the Buckeyes on an 80-yard, game-winning touchdown drive. With a little more than one minute remaining, he scored the winning touchdown on an option play that OSU ran before Wisconsin's defense could get set.

On and on it went as the Badgers dropped their first four conference games before finally beating Illinois. It was the first genuine rough stretch for Bielema. After the Badgers beat the Illini, Barry Alvarez said he made a point to congratulate Bret, telling him that he "became a coach today." What he meant was that every coach goes through a crisis when it seems as though your team gets no breaks and it appears the sky is falling. A coach's job is to get his team through such a stretch, and a victory against Illinois was a good sign.

But sometimes teams have more than a few bad weeks. Sometimes the season falls well short of expectations, and that was the case in 2008. In the final game of the regular season, Wisconsin needed overtime, and three missed extra points, to slip past FCS opponent Cal Poly. The Champs Sports Bowl was a mess with some Wisconsin and Florida State players engaging in some pregame jaw jacking. As the game progressed, there was little for the Badgers to say. The Seminoles dominated the game en route to a 42–13 victory.

Bret knew he had a talented team, but he also realized some of those talented players were not necessarily the right fit for his program. He made some difficult choices to remove a couple of young men from the team. Sometimes you add by subtracting.

By 2009, the Badgers were heading in the right direction. They were not quite championship material, but they certainly were a contender, and they were earning that status in the typical Wisconsin Way, by getting unheralded players who perform far beyond what many might have expected.

One of those players was defensive lineman O'Brien Schofield who blossomed as a senior, recording 12.5 sacks. A converted linebacker, Schofield became a force, getting two sacks at Ohio State and two more against 14th ranked Miami as the Badgers returned to the Champs Sports Bowl, and this time ended the season on a positive note, defeating the Hurricanes 20–14.

Playing the end opposite of Schofield was J.J. Watt, who in 2007 was a tight end at Central Michigan. The Pewaukee, Wisconsin, native wanted to play for his home state school. After leaving CMU, Watt earned some money by delivering pizzas. Within a couple of years, Watt went from delivering pizzas to delivering hits on opposing quarterbacks. During his redshirt transfer season of 2008, Bielema kept telling anyone who would listen about this former tight end turned defensive lineman who created havoc in practice. "Just wait until you see him next year," the head coach would say.

Bielema was right. In 2009 he was good. By 2010, Watt was nearly unstoppable, with 21 tackles for loss, three forced fumbles, three blocked kicks, one interception, and seven sacks, many in clutch situations. His motto "Dream Big–Work Hard" became very popular in Wisconsin. I would guess it is working rather well in Houston, too, as Watt had a sensational rookie season with the Texans.

Another overlooked player ended up being the 2009 Big Ten Freshman of the Year. For whatever reason, Ohio State, and nearly every other school in America, showed next to no interest in Chris Borland, a linebacker from Kettering, Ohio. At 5'11", perhaps the Buckeyes viewed him as being a tad undersized, but the Badgers liked what they saw from the freakishly athletic Borland. If the opposing team was guilty of a turnover, there was a good chance Borland had something to do with it. In his rookie year, he forced five fumbles and recovered three.

Borland also blocked a punt against Wofford that resulted in a touchdown, and in the final regular season game that year at Hawaii, the linebacker kicked three extra points. Unfortunately, the Rose Bowl season of 2010 was a disappointment for Borland personally, as shoulder trouble forced him to redshirt.

Then there was the quarterback. Scott Tolzien was another in a line of Wisconsin signal callers who worked under the radar. He was not exactly a national recruit, and while many figured Curt Phillips or perhaps Dustin Sherer would be the starting quarterback, Tolzien was proving to be the best fit for the job. His first pass of the 2009 season was an 80-yard touchdown strike to Issac Anderson.

The 2009 Big Ten Offensive Player of the Year was John Clay, who abused opposing defenses for 1,517 yards and 18 touchdowns. By the start of 2010, hopes were high for an even bigger year from the big tailback.

Clay ran well that fall, but as the year went along another back-field star emerged, helping Wisconsin become champions again.

Freshman James White played his way to Big Ten Freshman of the Year honors for 2010, leading the team in rushing with 1,052 yards. For a time, the Badgers had their own version of "Thunder and Lightning" with White and the bruising Clay. That combo was particularly effective in the rousing victory against top-ranked Ohio State, as the two combined for 179 yards and three touchdowns.

However, there was one Badger who left the building that evening wondering about his future at Wisconsin.

Montee Ball never left the bench that evening. His position coach, John Settle, referred to Ball as the proverbial "middle child" of the three tailbacks. The quickness of White plus the power of Clay meant very few opportunities for Ball, who thought perhaps he should ask the coaches to move him to linebacker.

It was another case of how sometimes in life the best moves are the ones you don't make.

Following the victory against Ohio State, the Badgers traveled to Iowa. Hopes were high in Iowa City, and with several attractive games at rowdy Kinnick Stadium that year, the recipe appeared to be good for a Hawkeyes title run.

The Wisconsin-Iowa game was a classic, but the Badgers were running out of players, especially at tailback. Clay and White were banged up. Clay continued, but White had to come out of the game. Enter Ball, who caught five passes and rushed three times for 18 yards, including the game-winning score with 1:06 to play.

The touchdown was possible because Bielema reached into his bag of tricks, and it worked perfectly against his alma mater. Facing a fourth down at the Badgers' own 26-yard line, Bielema called for a fake punt, and Brad Nortman had nothing but open space on a 17-yard run up the middle to keep the drive alive.

Ball's touchdown run had its own drama. At first glance, it appeared Iowa stopped him just short of the goal line. The football also popped out, and Hawkeyes fans were thinking fumble as Iowa recovered in the end zone to perhaps ice the game. After a replay review, however, two things fell into Wisconsin's favor. No, it was not a fumble, and Ball actually scored—giving the Badgers the lead and eventually the game.

For the rest of the season, Ball was a star. In the final five games, he rushed for 777 yards and 14 touchdowns. To say the least, that was just a preview of what was in store for 2011.

In the four games after Iowa, there was little in the way of drama. The Badgers started slowly at Purdue but pulled away in the second half. They torched Indiana 83–20. For me, a highlight was watching reserve quarterback Nate Tice score in the fourth quarter. A terrific young man, Tice rarely played, and I was excited to see him get into the end zone. However, I thought it would be best to try to temper my enthusiasm after I looked at the scoreboard. It hit me that Tice's run meant the Badgers broke 80, something I had never witnessed in person on the football field.

The title-clinching game was another rout—70–23 against Northwestern—and the Badgers were off to Pasadena for the first time since the 1999 season.

The tough part about the 2011 Rose Bowl with TCU was the fact that the Badgers simply were not as sharp as they had been down the stretch of the regular season. They also played a team that was just a bit better, led by quarterback Andy Dalton and an out-standing linebacking corps.

Still, the Badgers failed to make plays they had made most of the season. The defense struggled getting off the field. There were a couple of dropped passes or an open receiver not found. They did not play poorly, but as can happen in bowl games, sometimes the layoff affects some teams more than others. I believe the four-and-a-half weeks between games had at least something to do with Wisconsin's performance. Then again, as difficult as it might be for many to admit, perhaps they just lost to a better team that day.

It was a tough way for the Badgers to end that glorious season. In the postgame media session, Watt struggled to control his emotions. I felt bad for senior safety Jay Valai, who could only stand and watch as the confetti was flying and players from a school near his hometown were celebrating.

I thought Tolzien deserved better, but man, what a two-year run he had at Wisconsin. It is safe to assume that there was a short list of people who thought Scotty had the goods to be a starting quarterback in the Big Ten. Turns out he was a very good Big Ten quarterback. As a senior, he completed 73 percent of his passes for nearly 2,500 yards.

The numbers only tell part of the story. Off the field, he shared an apartment with offensive lineman John Moffitt and Bill Nagy. With Tolzien and Moffitt, it was the UW's version of *The Odd Couple.* To make a long story short, Tolzien comes across as very straight-laced. He likes everything to be in order. For Moffitt, not so much. It made for some entertaining interviews when Moffitt would complain that even with a quarterback as a roommate, it never helped the All-American lineman get any dates. Moffitt also joked that he would trash the apartment, just to get under Tolzien's skin. I am happy to report I never visited their apartment.

An even better story involving Tolzien had to do with his relationship with a boy named Jaxson Hinkens. In 2009, Hinkens was stricken with cancer. At the time of the diagnosis, Jaxson was 6 years old, and the outlook was very poor.

As Jaxson was going through chemotherapy, the family reached out to the UW football program. Jaxson's mom and dad were hoping that Tolzien would be able to spend a few minutes with their son. They said he spent nearly two hours with Jaxson, and a friendship began. There would be days when Tolzien would be late for some media interview requests. On more than one occasion, he was tardy with reporters because he was on the field playing catch with Jaxson or another child who was battling some type of illness.

The good news is Jaxson beat the cancer and was able to travel to the Rose Bowl to watch his favorite quarterback. The game might not have had an ideal outcome, but maybe Tolzien earned a big assist in helping a young man win a much more important contest.

There are several other student-athletes like Tolzien on the UW campus. In an era when there is plenty not to like about major college sports, people such as Scott Tolzien serve as a reminder of what is good about the game. The Badgers had returned to the philosophy of finding players who were the right fit for the school.

Just ask Jaxson Hinkens.

23

Russell Mania and Why I Don't Like Mary

IN HIS FIRST OFFICIAL PRACTICE as a Wisconsin Badger, Russell Wilson gave observers an idea that his skill level might be a little different from the norm. Keep in mind that in college football, players do not wear full gear for the first few practices, so rushing to judgment can be dangerous. Still, when the right-handed Wilson rolled to his left, then squared away and fired a 40-yard strike to hit the receiver between the numbers, a few of us just looked at each other and smiled.

The University of Wisconsin has had some very good quarterbacks. As the program grew in the last two decades, the Badgers have had some tough, better-than-advertised players at the position. They might not have always been very pretty, but signal callers such as Bevell, Samuel, Bollinger, Sorgi, Stocco, Donovan, and Tolzien were plenty good enough.

Yet Wilson got everyone's attention in a big hurry. The only knock on him is that he isn't 6'5". His listed height was 5'11", but as he often said, "I play on my toes, so I'm really taller than 5'11"."

It was difficult to disagree. He had very few passes deflected at the line of scrimmage, either in games or even during practice. He was physically and mentally strong, and he had great feet. As good as the offensive line was in 2011, Wilson's scrambling ability prevented numerous sacks.

Quarterbacks are judged in different ways, not the least of which is how they perform when the chips are down. I thought this was when Wilson was at his best. He finished ninth in the Heisman Trophy voting; had the Badgers been able to pull out victories at Michigan State and at Ohio State, I believe Wilson would have been invited to New York, and he might have won the thing.

In East Lansing, Wilson led the Badgers to a pair of fourth-quarter touchdowns to tie the game with a little more than one minute to play. It was the type of rally that Heisman voters love. But on the final play of regulation, Michigan State scored on a Hail Mary when Kirk Cousins heaved a deep pass that was deflected into the hands of receiver Keith Nichol, who fought his way just across the goal line for a game-winning score.

The following week at Ohio State, Wilson again worked his magic, taking the Badgers on two late-game scoring drives to give Wisconsin a 29–26 lead in the final minute. It was another Heisman Moment, but there was one more cruel plot twist—Braxton Miller's touchdown pass that I have mentioned enough already.

Some called it Hail Mary II. Wisconsin sports fans are not big fans of Mary.

Even in the Rose Bowl, Wilson very nearly produced what might have been the most dramatic ending in the rich history of that game. Starting at the UW 13 with 16 seconds to play, Wilson needed two plays to move the ball to the Oregon 25-yard line. With two seconds remaining, the Badgers tried to line up and spike the ball, but time ran out, ending the game. Had there been time for one more play, who knows what would have happened? We do know that had the Badgers scored a touchdown, Bret Bielema said he would have gone for two. The Badgers coach was not interested in overtime. Oh, what might have been!

With Russell Wilson on board, the Badgers were favored by many to win the Big Ten title and maybe even more. I thought any expectations beyond a conference title might have been a little too much, but as good as the Badgers offense had been the previous two seasons, the 2011 addition was the most exciting I had ever seen.

Yes, it was even more exciting than the Ron Dayne–led Badgers of the late 1990s. Do not get me wrong. The 1998 and '99 Badgers proved to be better teams, but I believe the fireworks the 2011 offense provided made it extra special to watch.

Clearly, Wilson made the Badgers better. Just as clearly, the talent surrounding Wilson made him a better quarterback. Receivers Nick Toon and Jared Abbrederis became standout players, as did tight end Jacob Pedersen. And Montee Ball ran wild with a whopping 1,923 yards and a total of 39 touchdowns, the latter number tied the NCAA single-season record set by Barry Sanders in 1988.

The man was amazing. Ball ran for all those yards, scored all those touchdowns, and never fumbled. Former Badgers and Green Bay Packers offensive lineman Mark Tauscher joined Mike Lucas and me for the radio broadcast of the final regular season game against Penn State. When we mentioned that little nugget, Tauscher did a double-take. He found it hard to believe that a running back with so many touches would never lose a fumble. Through his junior season, Ball either ran the football or caught a pass 617 times. His next lost fumble will be his first.

A couple of games from that season stand out for all the right reasons. The first was the conference opener against Nebraska. It marked the Cornhuskers first official Big Ten game, and I was able to get a grasp of what the sport means to the people of that state. Thousands of Nebraska fans made the trip to Madison for the historic event. It was a fun week for former Cornhuskers linebacker Barry Alvarez, who encouraged the addition of his alma mater as the league's twelfth member.

It was a big atmosphere. The game was pretty good, too, especially for the Badgers. After falling behind in the second quarter 14–7, Wisconsin ripped off 34 straight points. Among the highlights was a 46-yard touchdown pass from Wilson to Toon. For Nick, that was catch No. 132 of his career, one more than his father, Al, had in his outstanding college career. There is nothing like passing your dad on a long touchdown reception.

The first Big Ten Championship Game was in 2011. Wisconsin's rematch with Michigan State could very well be the title game by which all others are measured. Given the stakes, it might be the best football game I have had the privilege to call.

Indianapolis is the perfect city for such an event, and Lucas Oil Stadium is a jewel. For fans, Indy is ideal because once you park your car downtown, you won't need it again until you drive home. Everything is within walking distance. There are wonderful restaurants, sports bars, and everything else a fan enjoys.

As the years go by and more fans get to experience the excitement of a league championship game, Indianapolis will be up for grabs.

Yet I can still imagine what it will be like in 2020. Let us say Ohio State and Michigan have some amazing finish. I believe people still will say, "Yeah, it was a great game, but that first title game between Wisconsin and Michigan State was even better."

Badgers-Spartans II had it all. Montee Ball scored four touchdowns. Much like the first game between the two teams, Michigan State erupted in the second quarter, scoring 22 points. At the half, Sparty led 29–21. I have to admit I thought the Badgers had very little chance of winning. The matchup simply did not look good. The defense struggled to get off the field, and after a hot start the Wisconsin offense had stalled.

In the locker room, a couple of players went off, including defensive tackle Patrick Butrym. Normally a rather laid-back sort, Butrym had seen enough of Michigan State having its way at Wisconsin's expense.

"It's easy to be a leader when you are winning by 52 points," Butrym told reporters. "The thing I couldn't stand is having Michigan State guys with the roses in their mouths, prancing around the field."

Butrym admitted to perhaps stepping out of character but added, "Sometimes you need to be a jerk."

It was the perfect time to be a jerk.

In a shootout of a game, the Badgers held the Spartans' red-hot offense to 10 points in the second half. Still, Wisconsin was on the ropes in the final minutes. Facing a fourth-and-6 from the MSU 43, Russell Wilson struck again. Working from the shotgun, Wilson started to roll to his left, much like he did on that first day of practice in August. Only this time, he was facing pressure. Realizing he would be unable to run for the first down, Wilson stopped, squared up, and heaved a deep pass down the right side of the field. Waiting for it was Jeff Duckworth, who reached up and pulled down the ball against two Michigan State defenders. One play later from the Spartans' 7-yard line, Ball dashed into the end zone.

A two-point conversion pass from Wilson to Jacob Pedersen gave the Badgers a 42–39 lead. After forcing a Michigan State punt, Wisconsin was unable to run out the clock, giving MSU one final chance at victory.

However, just after Brad Nortman punted, Michigan State's Isaiah Lewis ran into him. To be sure, there was contract, but just to make sure, Nortman went down as though he was shot. That is exactly what punters are instructed to do.

Keshawn Martin returned the punt to the UW 3-yard line, but everyone in the house knew the play was coming back. On the air, I told our listeners, "I think that Michigan State ran into the punter, and if that's the case, that's the game."

It was the case. And it was the game.

For the Spartans, it was a bitter pill. For the Badgers, it was very, very sweet. In what has developed into a strong rivalry, the

Wisconsin Badgers made up for the Hail Mary Heartbreak with another classic game that went in their favor.

It was fun to witness. For a conference that has built its reputation largely on the tradition of programs such as Ohio State and Michigan, it should satisfy Badgers fans to know that in the inaugural Big Ten title game, it was the Wisconsin Badgers who stole the show.

Perhaps there are sexier college football programs, and that is okay. The current formula continues to work well. The Badgers have actually used their perceived lack of sexiness to their advantage. As center Peter Konz told me before the 2011 season began, "The media attention that's been building around us is nice. I've seen some articles saying that Wisconsin is a program on the rise. But there is still something essentially Wisconsin that says, 'Okay, we are still unproven. We are still like that working type.' None of us is a five-star [recruit]. We know that. We've still got something to prove."

As long as future Wisconsin teams embrace that mentality, I like the Badgers' chances of proving they can continue to roll with the big boys of college athletics.

Why not Wisconsin, indeed.

24

The Next Step?

CAN THE BADGERS WIN A NATIONAL TITLE in football and/or basketball? That is a rather popular question I get on the speaking circuit. No doubt Barry, Bret, and Bo get that inquiry every now and then.

Given the sustained success of those programs, I suppose it is a natural question. When your football team plays in 10 straight bowl games, including back-to-back Rose Bowls, and your basketball team has been an NCAA Tournament regular for more than a decade with multiple Sweet 16 appearances, it should surprise no one that some fans want a little bit more.

My fear is that fans will take winning for granted, as though it is some type of birthright. Some might refer to it as the Atlanta Braves Syndrome. This goes back to the 1990s when the Braves went from a largely irrelevant team to a perennial division winner and World Series contender. They did win it all one time, but after suffering through several years of great regular seasons only to see a post-season run fall short, fans were not so fast to flock to the ballpark.

So far, that has not been a major issue at Wisconsin. At times the crowds are pretty quiet, but the chairs usually are occupied. However, in December 2011 the Badgers hosted a good UNLV team, and a sportswriter from Las Vegas compared the Kohl Center atmosphere to a library. Actually the quote from Ed Graney's column in

217

the *Las Vegas Review Journal* was, "Libraries are more intimidating than this atmosphere."

Home-court advantage can work in mysterious ways. The Badgers won that day, thanks to sophomore guard Ben Brust, who made all seven of his three-point shots against the Runnin' Rebels. Can you credit the crowd for lulling UNLV to sleep?

Make no mistake, being a ticket-buying fan is getting more expensive by the year. Relatively speaking, the University of Wisconsin holds the line reasonably well, but attending UW football and basketball games is hardly cheap.

With higher donation requirements and the occasional ticket-price hike, a fan will have higher expectations. Not only does he want to win and win big, he also wants to be entertained along the way. Bring on the highlight reel dunks and the spectacular 80-yard touchdown passes and the tailback who can turn a routine play into a twisting and turning touchdown run.

This is where things can get dangerous for the Wisconsins of the world.

While I give Dick Bennett the credit for the phrase, "Know who you are," the fact is many of the coaches on the UW campus work by that philosophy, and the results have been positive.

The basketball team has had its stars—from Michael Finley, Devin Harris, Alando Tucker, and Jordan Taylor, among others. These are guys who make plays that fans talk about the next day at the office or even years later. They give Wisconsin an identity beyond the state's borders.

However, the heart and soul of the Badgers' success is their strict adherence to fundamentals. Dick Bennett was a stickler for them, and so is Bo Ryan. I often tell people a key to the Badgers' success is that they will "fundamental you to death." It's probably not the best word usage in the English language, but I believe I made my point.

Wisconsin's coaches believe it is more important to minimize mistakes than it is to make the *SportsCenter* Top 10 Plays of the Day.

Players learn the value of the shot fake. A guard learns how to score from the low post. If they want to play for Ryan, they understand his defensive rules, and they understand that every day in practice they will run through the same basic drills.

One of the best compliments an opponent can give, and Badger teams have heard it often, is that you have to beat them—the Badgers rarely beat themselves.

At times fans become impatient, wondering why other schools can recruit the five-star athlete who may only stay in school for one year—but oh, what a year it could be! I get it, but with rare exception, that is not the Wisconsin way. The method that has worked in Madison is to develop players, and many times by their junior and senior seasons, they become some of the better players in the Big Ten and beyond. The Badgers have done an excellent job of creating stars, not necessarily recruiting the instant difference maker. Keep in mind that Finley, Harris, Tucker, and Taylor were not targeted by many of the nation's top programs. They turned out to be okay, right?

There is nothing wrong with dreaming of a national title. It is dangerous to expect one. There is a difference. Is winning one possible? Of course it is, but even the best teams need a few breaks along the way.

In basketball, a good tournament draw certainly helps. In the Badgers' run to the 2000 Final Four, they played teams with loads of talent, but against Arizona and LSU they faced very young guards and were able to frustrate them. It did not hurt that Jon Bryant got red hot at just the right time of the year.

At the same time, in the national semi-finals, Wisconsin faced the worst possible opponent in Michigan State. Had it drawn Florida instead, I believe the result in Indianapolis could have been much different.

In 2007, Bo Ryan's team won 30 games and for one week in late February was ranked No. 1 in the nation. Then the Badgers lost at

Michigan State. In the following game at Ohio State, with a chance to win another Big Ten title, Brian Butch dislocated his elbow and the Badgers lost a heartbreaker. That team, which seemed to be in line for something extra special, ended up bowing out of the NCAA Tournament in the second round, suffering a six-point loss to UNLV.

Many teams, including the Badgers, can find it next to impossible to overcome a late-season injury to such an important player. Would Wisconsin have been a Final Four team with a healthy Brian Butch? Who knows? But it would have been fun to find out.

Think about what needs to happen for a so-called traditional power to go all the way. Michigan State has had one of the most consistent high-level programs in America. Tom Izzo has taken six of his teams to the Final Four, but he has *just* one national championship.

Ohio State has had loads of talent for many years, but the school's one and only national title was in 1960. Other power programs such as Syracuse and Arizona have one crown. The point here is that while winning an NCAA title is a worthy goal, defining a season as a success or a failure based on being the last team to cut down the nets is dangerous if not foolish.

As long as Wisconsin continues to make the NCAA field, anything can happen. The young talent on this team shows plenty of promise. The skill level is solid, and there is some play-making ability with young guards such as George Marshall. As long as they stick with the plan that has worked so well for Ryan's Badgers, there is always hope.

I will gladly accept having a chance most of the time rather than the "all in" for one year, then watching as a roster is gutted and a program sinks to mediocrity or worse. If that ever happens, you can guarantee that seats will become available.

• • •

Football is a similar animal, perhaps made even more challenging by the absence of a playoff, which is in line to change to a four-team postseason.

When Russell Wilson announced in June 2011 that he would play one more season of college ball at Wisconsin, even some national analysts were mentioning the Badgers as a national championship contender. I remember being at a UW-related golf outing the day of the announcement. Our group was at the turn, so we stopped at the clubhouse for a moment. On the TV screen was ESPN's Rod Gilmore, and he was singing the praises of Wilson. Others joined in, and the buzz in Madison got over the top in a big hurry.

I told someone that I already felt sorry for Russell. How could he live up to this hype? In retrospect, he probably surpassed expectations, if that is possible. He never had a bad game, and the offense broke records it set the previous year. But it was not quite enough to get the Badgers into the BCS title game.

Were they ever really a title contender? Yes, but they were also vulnerable. The secondary was young at a couple of positions, and the better offenses were able to exploit that. The special teams units had their ups and downs and paid a heavy price at times. It should be noted that about a dozen other teams were championship threats. You think Oregon would like to have another shot at USC? You think Oklahoma State would turn down a rematch with Iowa State? What about Boise State?

In college football, your team can do just about everything right and still be at the mercy of the computers. In the world of make-believe, let us say the 2011 Badgers went 12–0 in the regular season plus the Big Ten Championship Game. The computers, which make up one-third of the BCS rankings, were never very kind to Wisconsin. Would those numbers have been high enough to earn a Top 2 ranking, ahead of an Alabama team that had just one loss thanks to a three-point overtime setback to unbeaten LSU?

Maybe, but imagine the debate, not to mention the uproar, of the team that ended up third. You thought the Oklahoma State folks were mad after the 2011 season? I would guess that is nothing compared to the cries of fans in Wisconsin or Alabama at being left out of the big game.

When Barry Alvarez was building Rose Bowl championship teams, he often spoke of having five great players and at least being solid everywhere else on the field. With players such as Ron Dayne, Chris McIntosh, Wendell Bryant, Tom Burke, and Jamar Fletcher, Alvarez was able to lead the program to glory in the late 1990s. There was little if anything that was fancy about those teams, but they would "fundamental" you to death. That offense would pound the heck out of you, too.

After the back-to-back Rose Bowl title seasons of 1998 and 1999, Alvarez admitted that the staff strayed from its recruiting philosophy. The Badgers recruited a higher-caliber athlete and often ended up in second place. As a result, there were a few years when players hit the field before they were ready, and perhaps others might have been playing out of position. By 2001, the Badgers failed to make a bowl game, and in 2002 they needed to beat Minnesota on the final weekend of the regular season to become bowl eligible—with a 2–6 Big Ten record. Of course, that team went on to beat Colorado in the Alamo Bowl, so even in a so-called down year, the Badgers finished on a high note.

Forever to his credit, Barry recognized what happened in recruiting, and by his final season in 2005, the program was back on the upswing, culminating with a dominating performance against favored Auburn in the Capital One Bowl.

Bret Bielema would love nothing more than to bring a national title to Wisconsin. Yet he too understands the "know who you are" philosophy that has stood the test of time. Sure, he has had some stars—Wilson, Ball, J.J. Watt, and perhaps others who are emerging, such as Chris Borland and Mike Taylor. But the coach is more than willing to take a swing at the so-called big boys of college ball with his lunch-pail-toting, roll-up-your-sleeves-and-go-to-work bunch.

I think it would be very easy to fall into the trap of straying from a formula in a one-shot attempt at winning it all with the understanding that the following couple of years might be pretty rough. I call that trading tomorrow for today. At Wisconsin, I tend to believe that is a very high-risk tactic, and the consequences could be quite damaging.

What I like about the Badgers football and basketball programs is that every year, at worst, I believe they have a chance to be pretty good, and sometimes special. The foundation is in place with a group of players who, by and large, are excellent fits for the University of Wisconsin. With hard work and a little luck, perhaps they can recruit the extraordinary player, the one who can change a team from good to great.

That is far easier said than done, but with the Badgers' current plan it is certainly doable. A few exceptional players surrounded by solid contributors can equal lasting memories for fans. That is the formula that has worked at Wisconsin. Why try to fix something that isn't broken?

25

Thank You and Good Night

I WOULD KICK MYSELF if I did not give a little love to my fellow Big Ten radio broadcasters, many of whom I consider to be very good friends. Part of the enjoyment of this line of work is getting to know the voices of other schools. When we gather at the annual Big Ten Football Kickoff Luncheon or the conference basketball tournament, we try to get together to share stories and have a few laughs.

Probably my best friends on the circuit are Ohio State announcer Paul Keels and Iowa's Gary Dolphin. My boy Keels might have the best pure voice in sportscasting. Compared to him, a lot of us probably sound like Pee Wee Herman. Some of us call him the James Earl Jones of play-by-play guys, his pipes are that good.

Dolphin might be the funniest person I have met in this business. I swear everyone in Iowa knows him. A lot of people in Wisconsin do, too. Gary's wife, Cindy, is from Wisconsin and was a big Badger fan. Last summer some folks in Dubuque had a roast for Dolph. Among the roasters were Hayden Fry, Steve Alford, and Bret Bielema. I was unable to make it, but I recorded a few barbs directed Gary's way.

Bret took his fiancée (now wife, Jen) to the event, and I made mention of it. "Way to show Jen a good time Bret," I said. "Let's see—you told her, 'Hey honey, let's drive to Dubuque, Iowa, for an evening with Gary Dolphin! What a thrill.'"

With Keels, Dolphin, and myself, when two of the three are together, it is almost guaranteed a phone call will be made to the missing party, and the wisecracking will begin.

Northwestern's Dave Eanet and Penn State announcer Steve Jones also are good friends. Dave is known as Mr. Cat, and the NU alum has called some wild football games, several of which were against Wisconsin. As the sports director at WGN Radio in Chicago, Dave is one of the real good people in the industry.

The same can be said of Steve Jones. When the Sandusky story was breaking in State College last fall, I thought about Steve and how he was handling everything. That's how it works in this business. When something bad happens, not only do we think of those who are directly involved, we often wonder how our counterparts are doing. He handled it all very well—not that it could have been easy. Steve teaches a sportscasting class at Penn State, which is something I have thought about doing here in Madison. Maybe one day. Then again, maybe I should enroll at Penn State and take one of Steve's classes.

Indiana's Don Fischer is a pro's pro. He is a 25-time Indiana Sportscaster of the Year, which makes us wonder why they don't just name the award after him? Don has worked with coaches such as Bob Knight, Mike Davis, Kelvin Sampson, and now Tom Crean. Through it all, Don has held up extremely well. He has called the greatest moments in IU hoops history, including three national championship seasons. Don also is an avid golfer. Unlike me, he is very good.

The bottom line is that they are all good guys. Michigan State's Will Tieman and George Blaha, Michigan's Frank Beckman and Matt Shepard, Minnesota's Mike Grimm, Purdue broadcasters Larry "The Cliz" Clisby and Tim Newton, and Illinois voice Brian Barnhart. Nebraska is a newbie to the Big Ten, but I hear nothing but good things regarding Greg Sharpe and Kent Pavelka.

I would be remiss if I did not mention our honorary Big Ten brother, Wes Durham, the radio voice of Georgia Tech and the

Atlanta Falcons. A few of us in the league have gotten to know him, mostly because the teams we cover sometimes play in the same city during the NCAA Tournament, or perhaps some of us will hook up with him during the Big Ten/ACC Challenge. In the spring of 2011, Wes' father, Woody, retired after an amazing run as the voice of the North Carolina Tar Heels. If the Big Ten expands again, Keels, Dolphin, Fischer, and I will all put in a good word for the Georgia Tech Yellow Jackets!

On the Badger Sports Network, I have never been crazy about being called "The Voice." Actually, I am just *a* voice. We have several. Brian Posick is an NHL-good hockey announcer who has called many thrilling Badgers games, including the NCAA title run by Mike Eaves' squad in 2006. Mike Heller handles UW women's basketball, and Jon Arias does the same for the Badger volleyball team.

My broadcast partner, Mike Lucas, must believe that sleep is overrated. In addition to his analyst duties for football and basketball, he hosts a weekday morning show on Madison radio station WTSO from 6:00 to 8:00 AM. (I join him for the second hour. That is early enough for me.) He also writes for the athletic department website, which includes an impressive-looking online magazine called *Varsity*. In addition, he hosts a 30-minute TV show, *Sidelines*, which is a roundtable program where Mike and his guests discuss the week's sports topics in Wisconsin.

Like I said, the man must not like to sleep.

Our football and men's basketball engineer is Dave McCann, who juggles the chore of keeping us on the air while editing highlights for the athletic department website, uwbadgers.com, the coaches' TV shows, and whatever else is needed on a given day or night.

The growth of University of Wisconsin athletics also includes sales and marketing. Badger Sports Properties, a division of Learfield Sports, handles the multi-media duties. When Learfield first acquired the rights, it was a radio-only endeavor. Now it is a major operation that also includes some television, website sales, stadium and arena signage, and much, much more. Our general manager is Jeff Jurgella, who has been very supportive and willing to help the radio folks whenever possible.

The same goes for the folks at UW athletic communications. People such as Brian Lucas, Patrick Herb, Brian Mason, and Karl Anderson do much of the behind-the-scenes work that makes life easier for us broadcasters. We even use Patrick as our sideline analyst for the football broadcasts.

A special mention goes to UW Senior Associate Athletic Director Justin Doherty, who provided me with some valuable feedback as I made my first attempt at writing a book.

On a more personal note, I am blessed beyond belief to have wonderful parents. My love of sports comes from my father, Sal. He said that when I was a small child, I sat with him and watched an entire baseball game on TV. It was past my bedtime, but he could tell I was riveted by the game, so he let me stay up late. Some of my fondest memories are of the two of us driving to old Riverfront Stadium to watch the Cincinnati Reds.

I am grateful that neither my father nor my mother, Lee, ever discouraged me from pursuing this type of career. To be brutally honest, small-market broadcasting salaries are awful. Some parents would push their children to do something else, preferably something that paid reasonably well. My mom and dad knew this was something I dearly wanted to do for a living, so they let me run with it. I do not get to see them nearly enough, but at least they can hear the games, and I know of at least two people in Dayton, Ohio, who have become loyal Badger fans.

I owe a big thank you to all the players and coaches at the University of Wisconsin. At any number of functions, I have happily pointed out that those who play for the Badgers tend to be easy to root for. With rare exceptions, the UW student-athlete is a polite, cooperative individual who represents the university the right way. The coaches demand nothing less.

I believe that still matters to fans in this state. Sure, everyone wants to win one more game or one more trophy, but in Wisconsin, the bottom line isn't always the number of victories. How they win is important, as well. Yes, sometimes they get knocked down, but they always get back on their feet. It is part of what makes this such a good story.

Finally, thanks to Badgers fans everywhere. For several years, the UW has been among the nation's leaders in attendance for football, men's basketball, hockey, and volleyball. In this bumpy economy, the loyalty of fans in this state is a sight to behold.

Even in the down years, there would be a hard-core group of Badgers backers who would get to as many games as possible, both home and away. I enjoy sitting back and watching how much these fans love their team and how happy they are when Wisconsin wins a big game.

The University of Wisconsin programs have come a long way from that September day in 1993 when Joe Panos asked the question, "Why not Wisconsin?" On that day, Joe's comments were strictly about football. As it turns out, those words mean so much more. It is not so much a question as it is a philosophy, a way to tell the world that the Wisconsin Badgers matter.

In the last 20-plus years, the Wisconsin Badgers have enjoyed one fantastic ride. Some have said these are the good old days. If that is true, let us hope they continue for many years to come.

Why not?

Epilogue:
Mrs. Lepay's Forum

by Linda Lepay

CONGRATULATIONS! By making it to the end of the book, you've helped settle a bet. Matt didn't think anyone would read this far without being bored into a stupor. He imagined most people would use this book as a beer coaster or a kitchen trivet. But we know better, don't we?

When Matt agreed to write this book, I offered to pen the last chapter. I enjoy writing humor, and Matt has been a source of amusement to me for years. You probably think of him in his professional life, yet I get to see those private times when he thinks he's being funny and when he thinks he's being deadly serious, which are some of his funniest moments.

This chapter is the second version of the Epilogue or v.2.0. V.1.0 is a never-to-be-seen missive where I crafted a loving tribute to my husband. I told stories that showed Matt being uniquely Matt—from his work ethic to his low-key demeanor. It didn't seem right for him to put so much effort into this book only to have Chuckles the Wife pull up the clown car at the end for some laughs at his expense.

I don't think I exhaled while he flipped through v.1.0. When he got to the end, he stacked the pages neatly together and put it down.

"It's sweet," he said.

Sweet?! Newborn lambs are sweet. Marshmallow chicks are sweet until Easter is over and they turn into candy bricks. No one had ever described my writing as sweet. Snarky, yes. Insightful, of course. But sweet?

We didn't talk about the chapter for a few days. Then he started to recommend edits—not to correct inaccuracies but to tone down the praise I had heaped on him. V.1.0 had too much cheerleading and not enough laughs. "Show me warts and all," he said.

It's like I'd been given Warren Buffett's Nordstrom credit card. Can you hear me cracking my knuckles in anticipation?

So I bring you:

The Epilogue: V.2.0—Matt the Wart

We met in college through a mutual friend in 1984. I'd like to say it was at a library dedication or a production of the spring dance recital. Instead it was at an Ohio State campus bar named Surf City (may it rest in peace). Our friend, Jon, was a journalism major who invited my roommate and me to hang out with his J-school buddies. One of those buddies sported jet black hair and a vicious mustache. I decided right away that I owed it to myself to meet Mr. 'Stache.

The 'Stache was a dedicated broadcast journalism major who aspired to be a sportscaster. I was impressed with his career focus since I had changed my own major three times. We were both seniors and appeared to be pretty set on our next steps after college: me, to grad school (where the undecided go to procrastinate), and Matt to a life of minimum-wage radio jobs. And we managed to do those things until fate intervened in 1988 with Matt's job offer in Madison, Wisconsin.

Fast forward nearly 25 years and he's written a book about his career. And fortunately, I have the opportunity to get in the last word. Heh, heh, heh.

Matt has certain rules he lives by—not on purpose, but he can't help himself. For example, if we're entering a building he'll open the door for me and then hold the door for the next 25 people. He's so polite that I call him America's Doorman. There are other rules he lives by. I like to call them "Mattisms."

Mattism No. 1: Never draw attention to yourself—or—don't gush, even when you meet your heroes.

In 2006, Matt won the Wisconsin Sportscaster of the Year award for the fifth time. We went to North Carolina for the awards ceremony. Legendary Cincinnati Reds radio announcer Marty Brennaman was inducted into the Hall of Fame that night. Matt grew up listening to Marty, and as a child, Matt thought Marty had the best job in the world. Finally, Matt was in the same room with the person who inspired him to get into the business.

"Go talk to him," I urged. "I'll take your picture."

"Maybe," he said. "I'm sure he's busy talking to other people."

I used all my herding skills to get the two of them in the same general area. I don't know if Matt would have introduced himself if I hadn't been such a nag. But a photo of Marty and Matt sits in Matt's office today. So give a point to the nag. I'm sure Matt still feels guilty for interrupting Marty's evening.

Mattism No. 2: Never cheer in the press box. Or in your house. Or during any sporting event.

Watching a sporting event with Matt is like watching a game in a monastery. There is limited chatting and no yelling. Matt's entire career has been about observing sporting events. It's less about being a fan and more about watching. That becomes annoying when I want to get into the spirit of the game.

Super Bowl XXXI was a huge day for Packers fans. We were invited to a friend's house for a party. Matt doesn't enjoy attending parties during sporting events. The chatter and party atmosphere disrupts his viewing experience. Up to that point I had watched almost zero minutes of Packers football that season. (Please be kind. I was still learning about Packer-dom.) But the mood was festive, and everyone was jazzed up. Plus, for me, a game on TV doesn't ruin a good party.

Here's me at a party: mingle, mingle, chatter, eat, quick glance at TV, more chatter.

Here's Matt at a party: sit in a chair, stare at TV, make no sound.

Remember when Reggie White sacked New England quarterback Drew Bledsoe?

The entire room was on its feet. Even I was fist-pumping and cheering as I turned to look at my spouse, who was still quietly sitting.

I frowned. "What are you doing?"

"What are *you* doing?" he replied. He smirked at me.

This is how someone in his profession watches sports. All those years of sitting in the press box had transformed Matt from the rabid sports fan I met in college to the professional killjoy he is now.

The Reds could win the World Series, the Super Bowl, and the Stanley Cup all at the same time, and he'd quietly nod his head.

Mattism No. 3: You can never prepare enough.

Let me set the scene for you. It's October and I'm home alone because the Badgers football team has a road game. I decide to watch some TV, but the DVR is recording a Big 10 game. If I change the channel, it will cancel the recording. Okay, fine. I'll go downstairs and watch that TV—except it is also recording a game. In fact, our two DVRs are so full of football games that I can barely record *30 Rock* without tipping the delicate balance of Matt's game preparation rituals.

People ask me how Matt prepares for games. Immersion. There is a complete focus on the next game, including attending endless practices, watching game tape, studying the media guide, and memorizing player numbers and statistics.

I know that his extensive preparation is what makes him successful. During "The Season" (August-April), his mind is on all things Badgers. Don't ask him a current-events question because he has no clue. He vaguely knows about a show called American Idol and thinks Jersey Shore is a place where people go on vacation.

Matt, like his sportscasting brethren, puts in ridiculous hours. He does not just show up for the game. During the season he will work from the moment he opens his eyes until his head hits the pillow at night. (Matt's note: She is stretching the truth here a little.) Most of the time this doesn't bother me—most of the time. Do you celebrate the holidays in November and December? Matt barely knows they are occurring. Thanksgiving tournaments mean he may not be home. Basketball plays games in late December. The football team goes to bowl games. I've spent many holidays without my spouse. Am I whining? Yes.

You know it's bad when every year Matt asks if I'm working on Memorial Day/Fourth of July/insert holiday here. Yes, dear, most Americans get holidays off. In return for this luxury I sit in a cubicle, so maybe he has the better deal.

Mattism No. 4: Never put off until tomorrow what you can get done in advance.

Procrastination is a mantra to me. Not so for my husband. And perhaps this is where we are the most different. Matt is always working ahead and checking things off his to-do list. I, on the other hand, love to make a list so I can ignore it. I've always put things off, opting for the last-minute thrill when something gets done just in time.

Matt thinks I'm crazy because this isn't how adults should act. I think he's a goody-goody who wants a gold star on his forehead. Take this book, for instance. Matt has been working on this manuscript in a steady manner for months. My only job was to write the epilogue. He is done with his 70,000+ words while I'm still playing around with my measly chapter.

It's true that we marry those who have characteristics that we lack. Part of the Yin and Yang of marriage is to appreciate what your partner brings to the table. So I try not to complain about his need to get things done and stay on schedule. I'm not a slacker (I'm not!), I just have a different appreciation of the time-space continuum.

My outlook on timeliness does at times collide with his promptness. I had the great opportunity to travel with Matt to the Rose Bowl a couple years ago. My marching orders were to be ready to leave the house by 9:00. What I heard was, "Be ready to leave at 9:00 AM." At 8:50 Matt was staring at me, coat and gloves on, car keys in hand. He was annoyed, and I was confused. I learned that day that Badgers football likes to be early for most things, especially travel. If one is even a little late, one may be left behind. "I work in the corporate world," I tried to explain as we drove to campus that day. "Someone who is five minutes early for a meeting is a dweeb." He stared ahead as if I wasn't there. Eeesh, I get it. Be early. Lesson learned.

Now that we've covered the Mattisms, there are a couple more stories I want to share about America's Doorman.

Freak Show

As I got to know Matt's college friends, who also had play-by-play aspirations, I found a common theme. They were freakishly devoted to the profession and had long-held beliefs that this was the job for them. You could say they had a calling to the job. In Matt's case, the broadcasting bug hit him quite young.

When Matt was eight years old, he would play with his electric football game. If you're over 45, you know what I'm talking about. The green metal surface was the field, while the players were plastic with a magnet on the bottom. The field vibrated and this is how your players allegedly moved (usually in circles). I have no idea how one threw a pass, but that's a topic for another day. While Matt's friends ran a play, Matt described the action. He also inserted commercials to make the game as authentic as possible. His mom says that Matt could be heard from his bedroom calling a game. This was perfectly acceptable behavior for a child. Little did anyone think at the time that he would never outgrow this phase.

Matt's parents still have his precious electric football game and they keep it safe. This is a good thing since it would have been recycled a long time ago had it made the move to Wisconsin.

Breaking Bread with Costas and Michaels

As you've read, Matt's job allows him to have brushes with sports greatness. But one evening we had unexpected pizza and beers with sportscasting royalty.

In 1997 Matt won the Wisconsin Sportscaster of the Year award for the first time. We went to North Carolina for the awards ceremony where each state winner was called on stage to receive his or her hardware. Handing out the awards was Bob Costas, the national winner that year. Also in attendance was Al Michaels, who won the Hall of Fame award.

The ceremony is held each year in Salisbury, North Carolina, a quaint Civil War–era town north of Charlotte. The town lacks a strong night life, so we found ourselves back at the hotel wanting a beverage and maybe an evening snack.

As we headed to the lobby to determine our options, Bob Costas was looking at us.

"Do you guys want pizza?" he asked.

Matt and I spun around to see who he was talking to. There was no one behind us. Could it be that Bob Costas wanted to know if we were hungry?

"Sure," Matt said.

Costas and Michaels had taken custody of the lobby. Sprinkled amongst the legends were various state winners and their stunned spouses. We, or rather they, spent the evening chatting about the business and sports in general. Matt played it cool. I kept trying to make eye contact in a can-you-believe-this manner.

The guys were nice, funny, and highly entertaining, especially Costas, who easily mingled with everyone.

That night we learned the difference between high-profile national media and their less-famous brethren at the state level. Michaels and Costas got into a discussion about whether the Ritz Carlton or the Four Seasons was a better hotel.

Matt leaned into me and mumbled, "Fortunately, I don't have that problem in West Lafayette."

I had trouble falling asleep that night as I thought about such a casual gathering with freaking Bob Costas and Al Michaels. Who would believe me when we got home?

To borrow from Frank Capra, it's been a wonderful life. When I met this man many years ago, we had no idea that our adventures would include Badgers, Rose Bowls, cheeseheads, and long Wisconsin winters. We also never imagined we would have such close friendships with fans whose football team trounced the Buckeyes so many times. Okay, Matt could not care less about this last point. However, the heartburn lingered with me for many years.

By reading this book, you've had a chance to peek into Matt's professional life. And you've been able to listen to me explain that he's occasionally a wart, a freak, and a killjoy. But he has a job like few others. Wisconsin has been very good to us. Even I can appreciate that on the occasional New Years Eve when I'm home alone with the cats.

Sources

THANK YOU TO THE UNIVERSITY OF WISCONSIN Athletic Communications staff, led by Brian Lucas, for allowing me to plow through file after file of game programs, stat sheets, as well as old media guides and fact books. While a fair amount of material comes from my own collection of game broadcast recordings and archived interviews (courtesy of the Badger Sports Network, WTSO Radio, and Clear Channel Madison), it also was helpful to look back at some old newspaper articles. That was where the *Wisconsin State Journal*, the *Capital Times*, and the *Milwaukee Journal Sentinel* came in handy. I should also mention the pre-merger days of the Milwaukee newspaper industry, when the *Sentinel* and the *Journal* were fierce competitors.

The Internet age has made it more manageable to look up some old stories and stats. UWbadgers.com, madison.com, and jsonline. com are wonderful resources.

In addition, other recent books on University of Wisconsin athletics such as *Always a Badger: The Pat Richter Story*, *Don't Flinch*, *Another Hill to Climb*, and *The Dayne Game* helped to refresh my memory on a few stories.

Index